D0681309

MoviePlus X5 User Guide

How to Contact Us

Our main office (UK, Europe):	The Software Centre PO Box 2000, Nottingham, NG11 7GW, UK
Main:	(0115) 914 2000
Registration (UK only):	(0800) 376 1989
Sales (UK only):	(0800) 376 7070
Customer Service/ Technical Support:	http://www.support.serif.com/
General Fax:	(0115) 914 2020

North American office (USA, Canada):	Serif Inc, The Software Center, 17 Hampshire Drive, Suites 1 & 2, Hudson, NH 03051, USA
Main:	(603) 889-8650
Registration:	(800) 794-6876
Sales:	(800) 55-SERIF or 557-3743
Customer Service/ Technical Support:	http://www.support.serif.com/
General Fax:	(603) 889-1127

Online

Visit us on the web at:	http://www.serif.com/

International

Please contact your local distributor/dealer. For further details, please contact us at one of our phone numbers above.

Credits

Contents

Contents

1 Welcome

Welcome to MoviePlus X5!

Welcome to **MoviePlus X5**, the powerful video-editing program from Serif. MoviePlus is the program of choice for video editors looking for easy and intuitive ways to create and share their own movies.

MoviePlus X5 offers an exciting experience at all the key steps of movie creation—from importing media, media management (trimming and scene detection), and video editing, through to exporting your project to DVD and Blu-ray disc, as well as to YouTube, movie file, Apple devices, or PSP.

Video editing can be performed in **storyboard** or **timeline** mode (for ease-of-use vs. editing power). Whichever mode you plan to work in, you'll be the envy of your audience at your movie's first screening!

For a more detailed summary of what MoviePlus can offer, see **Key features** (p. 4).

Upgrading?

If you've upgraded from a previous version, this new edition of MoviePlus includes a host of **exciting new features** (p. 10) which keeps MoviePlus ahead of its competitors and at a fraction of the price!

Registration

Don't forget to register your new copy, using the **Registration Wizard** on the **Help** menu. That way, we can keep you informed of new developments and future upgrades!

Key features

Gathering and managing media

- **Import Media**
  Copy from **camcorder**, **USB mass storage devices (hard drive,
  memory stick/card, flash drives)**, or **CD/DVD**. MoviePlus transfers
  media files straight from your device, ready for use in your Media
  pane.

- **Trimming**
  Trim video clips to your preferred length in a dedicated **Trim** dialog,
  without affecting your original video clip.

- **Media Pane**
  Your project's media (video, image, and audio files) can be gathered
  together in a Media pane before commitment to your storyboard (or
  timeline). You can reuse media for subsequent projects by adding to
  the pane's Library tab. Fix incorrectly oriented image and video files by
  one-click rotation.

- **Quick Sourcing of Video, Audio, Image Content**
  Capture video and audio directly from sources like a DV (digital
  video) camcorder and video capture card. Take images straight off
  your camera.

- **Automatic Scene Detection and Management**
  Detect and utilize scenes within movies from tape-based camcorders
  (even adjust detection sensitivity). Exclude unwanted scenes, merge
  scenes together, or even add manual cuts to trim and split scenes to
  your liking! The original file is left intact, not split into pieces by the
  process.

MoviePlus basics

- **Storyboard Simplicity or Timeline Editing Power!**
  Use the Storyboard for basic movie projects or "slideshow" image montages. Clips are automatically arranged in sequence one-by-one with inter-clip transitions. The Timeline lets you arrange video and audio clips with editing freedom, working with an unlimited number of video and audio tracks (or groups).

Timeline essentials

- **Tracks and Groups**
  Store clips across multiple "layered" **tracks** for stunning **blending** effects (opacity control) or **split-screens**, **spins**, **rotations**, and **rolls** (transform control). Control opacity and transforms at group level using **video groups** (containing multiple video tracks).

- **Clip-based Opacity, Crop, and Transform Control**
  Apply opacity, cropping, and transforms to any selected clip!

- **Keyframe Controls**
  Transitions, effects, transforms, opacity, plus audio volume and stereo panning are all "key-framable". You can specify changes over time and all the in-between steps are calculated for you. The changes themselves can also adopt different speeds or accelerations by changing the keyframe properties.

- **Preset Envelopes**
  Using MoviePlus's advanced keyframe technology is even more accessible through a comprehensive range of preset envelopes—these can be simply dragged and dropped onto video and audio tracks and will perform previously complex video editing techniques, such as opacity, transform and crop, with ease.

- **Transparent Overlays**
  All of MoviePlus's video tracks support video transparency to superimpose not just titles but any 32-bit transparent image (or video) over your movie's action. Make portions of existing video transparent

by adding a mask (as you might in a bitmap-editing program like Serif PhotoPlus) or by picking a solid colour to become transparent. Use popular Blend Modes to adjust how your layered videos' pixels interact with each other.

- **Multiple Picture-in-Picture**
  Create professional picture-in-picture effects using video clips or still frames by easily editing the size and position of your video in the Video Preview pane. Perfect for showing supplemental visuals without detracting from the main movie, or tiling multiple videos together for a dynamic scene.

Audio

- **Audio Levels**
  Avoid audio distortion with the Levels meter—audio level meters indicate if your current audio levels hit the Red. Use as a master control volume to normalize project audio levels prior to movie export. Audio waveforms for any audio clip are optionally displayed on the timeline to help synchronize audio events.

- **Narration Recording**
  Record voice-overs while you play back your movie—simply set up your microphone, press record and begin talking!

- **Digital CD Ripping**
  Rip your audio CDs—great for creating movie soundtracks from your favourite songs.

- **Dolby® Digital Stereo Support**
  For DVD/Blu-ray disc export, MoviePlus now uses Dolby Digital to encode and compress audio (leaving more room for video!). Video files with Dolby Digital streams can also import without the need for third party codecs.

Text

- **In-Place Text Editing**
  Add **titles**, **captions**, and **credits** as separate text clips or as overlaid text ("floating" over your video).

- **Text Styles**
  For titles, captions, and credits, the new Text Styles gallery offers hand-picked styles for that professional look. Apply a full range of character formatting for custom text styles.

- **Text Animation**
  Bring text to life by choosing In and/or Out animations, all from the Galleries pane. Fly, Spin, Blinds, Explode, and Type are among an impressive collection of preset categories.

Transitions, CG Clips, and Effects

- **Cool Transitions**
  Automatic transitions between two clips make MoviePlus a breeze. MoviePlus offers dozens of built-in, customizable transitions allowing you to use standard transitions like wipes and cross-fades through to stretches, pushes, pixellation, and 3D transitions.

- **Computer Generated (CG) clips**
  For movie interludes or backdrops to titles or credits, add coloured **Backgrounds** (solid or gradient fills) or **Images** and **QuickShapes** such as hearts, chevrons, teardrops, and zigzags (plus many more). QuickShapes are also great for masking effects!

- **Stunning Video Effects**
  Enhance your movies with a wide range of customizable correction filters—pick from brightness, contrast, gamma adjustments, sharpen, and many more! Special effects include Old Film, Motion Blur, Mask, Noise, and Chroma Key. 2D filter effects, as well as **3D lighting** and **surface effects** are supported. Apply individually or cumulatively. Even perform reverse video playback as a special effect.

- **Audio Effects**
  Choose from a range of audio special effects—Reverb, Bass, Fill Left, Fill Right channel-related effects. Even use third-party VST effect plug-ins.

Performance

- **Pre-Rendering for Improved Video Playback**
  Render transitions, video clips, or a time range in the background for improved preview performance; lightning fast previews for complex timelines or clips with processor-intensive effects!

Ease of Use

- **Easy-to-use Panes**
  Enjoy larger and more intuitive panes which can float and be resized—design your own MoviePlus workspace! Make use of full screen previews on additional monitors.

- **Editing Toolbars for More Efficiency**
  Context-sensitive toolbars for storyboard and timeline; toolbars only offer the tools you need, when you need them.

- **Edit Multiple Attributes**
  Change individual, specific, or all attributes (e.g. transitions, clip durations) at the same time.

- **Switch Editing Modes**
  Swap between the simplicity of the storyboard and the editing power of the timeline. A single click gives an easy jump between either mode.

Exporting

- **Easy Exporting**
  Export to any media, file or device using either **Basic** or **Advanced** mode—the former uses unchanged project settings, the latter lets you modify project settings for export in a custom export template, which can be saved.

- **Share Worldwide with YouTube**
  Export your movie then automatically upload to your YouTube account.

- **PSP/iPod Export**
  Export mp4 movies to play on these popular devices. Upload to PSP directly from MoviePlus; import movie into iTunes for later syncing with iPods.

- **Built-in DVD Authoring!**
  Bring your movies to the masses with quick and easy authoring to disc (includes auto-erase)!

- **DVD Menu Designer**
  For handy chapter navigation, the **Menu Designer** lets you create your very own menu designs from a diverse range of pre-built templates, by changing layout, background images/music, titling, and button styles. The designer now offers DVD **Preview** (with remote control simulator), video menu backgrounds, and manual positioning of menu buttons. For multi-page menus, each page can adopt its own appearance (e.g., layout, background, etc).

New features

General

- **Multi-trimming and splitting** (p. 34)
  Create separate trimmed scenes per clip, removing unwanted video or audio content with ease—perform via Media pane, timeline or storyboard using the Trim dialog. Optionally, just **split (cut)** your clip up into multiple scenes! **Preview** each created scene and re-trim within the dialog. **Scene slipping** lets you change underlying content, while keeping the same trimmed clip duration.

- **Guides for Fine Positioning**
  Use for laying out your titles, images, shapes, and transform envelopes on your clips. Guides are for display only, helping you arrange clips and objects, and can be positioned either by drag-and-drop or dialog.

- **View in Full Screen!** (p. 39)
  Make use of all your monitor workspace with **Full Screen display**, equipped with pop-up transport controls!

- **Images and QuickShapes for Enhanced Movie Titles** (p. 180)
  Combine images, QuickShapes, and text together in your text clip's layout! Optionally, set your default text style for future text clips.

Ease of use

- **Easy Project Setup** (p. 20)
  From the Startup Wizard and Media pane, importing media options (**Import** and **Copy from Device**) offer to set up your project according to the chosen media clip's properties. For example, import a clip from your HD camcorder, and your project is set up as an HD project automatically!

- **Customized Keyboard Shortcuts, Menus, and Toolbars**
  Take advantage of customizable keyboard shortcuts—assign your own
  keystrokes to toolbar and menu commands! Tailor MoviePlus to your
  needs with menu, toolbar, and icon customization.

Performance

- **Background Task Management** (p. 207)
  For uninterrupted project development, **pre-rendering** and **proxy** file
  generation are now background tasks. Prioritize or delete any
  background tasks in **Background Task Manager**. For example,
  prioritize a proxy task for a specific HD video clip to complete ahead
  of other tasks.

- **Helper File Manager** (p. 212)
  Monitor, manage, and remove helper files used for pre-render
  preview, proxies, indexing, scene detection, waveform generation, and
  motion control. Allocate disk space thresholds for automatic helper
  file deletion—avoid running out of disk space ever again!

Effects

- **Video Noise Reduction** (p. 136)
  Use MoviePlus's Noise Reduction video effect to minimize the effects
  of luminance and chroma noise in your video clips.

- **Image Stabilization** (p. 136)
  The Stabilize effect eliminates unwanted camera shake present in your
  video clip.

Timeline

- **Overlay Links** (p. 81)
  Keep control of **caption titles**, **credits**, or **video overlays** by linking to
  your underlying clip—your overlay will be trimmed and moved as you
  trim or move your clip.

- **Clip Grouping** (p. 81)
  Select multiple clips along your track and then group together—great for making permanent associations between clips for bulk control, e.g. when moving multiple clips simultaneously or simply when keeping related content together.

- **Clip Overlap** (p. 105)
  Control the extent of overlapping between clips. Use for uniformly overlapping multiple clips by the same amount.

- **On-demand Waveform Generation** (p. 154)
  Create waveforms for audio clips just when you need them. Alternatively, generate waveforms in your Media pane before committing to your timeline—ideal if you're working with many audio clips.

Sharing via Discs

- **Create Blu-ray Discs!** (p. 188)
  With MoviePlus you can create and share your completed project via **Blu-ray discs**.

- **AVCHD on DVD** (p. 188)
  Export your HD project (AVCHD) to DVD, either taking advantage of cheaper media costs (compared to Blu-ray discs) or if you've not quite purchased a Blu-ray writer!

- **Multi-level Disc Menus** (p. 196)
  Create tiered disc menus, typically a main Titles menu (including Play Movie) and a subsidiary scene selection menu.

Importing/exporting

- **Import media via Media pane's Explorer tab** (p. 25)
  Access your computer's drives and folders directly from the **Explorer pane** and import media straight to the storyboard or timeline.

- **Export to all the latest Apple devices** (p. 199)
  Share your movie via your Apple iPad, iPhone, or iPod Touch.

Other improvements

- **Media pane improvements** (p. 27)
  Easily **locate media files** already on your storyboard/timeline (indicated by green check mark). Filter by **file type** in your Media pane—view only videos, images, or audio. Detailed view displays **frame size/rate**, with the option to display **pixel aspect ratio, interlace** method, **bit depth**, and more. **Sort** your media file list by column.

- **Logical Clip Addition to Tracks** (p. 72)
  Linked video and audio clips always "snap" into adjacent video and audio tracks when adding to the timeline.

- **Alter Duration of your Transitions** (p. 104)
  In timeline mode, change the duration of one or more transitions on your timeline.

- **Live Timeline Rippling** (p. 83)
  Automatic rippling takes place as you move clips by dragging. Existing clip overlaps are maintained when inserting clips, deleting clips, and editing clip/transition durations.

- **Pane layout control** (p. 36)
  Use buttons to maximize your Video Preview Pane or close the How To tab for maximizing your workspace area.

- **Background fills for text** (p. 176)
  Change the background to your text clips to any solid or gradient fill.

Licensed feature unlocking

As part of the MoviePlus import or export process, a new feature may have to be unlocked—this is purely for Serif licensing reasons and does not incur any charge. If a feature needs to be unlocked, MoviePlus will connect to the internet to automatically unlock it. If the automatic feature unlock fails (i.e., if there is no Internet connection) you will be prompted to that effect, then you can manually unlock the feature (see MoviePlus Help for details).

Once unlocked, the MoviePlus feature will be freely available and will not need unlocking again on your computer.

 In unlocking, Serif does not gather personal information from your computer, or any other information that may impinge confidentiality.

Installation

System requirements

- Windows-based PC with DVD drive and mouse.

- Microsoft Windows® XP (32 bit), Windows® Vista, or Windows® 7 operating system

- 1GB RAM

- 1.47GB free hard drive space*

- 1024 x 768 monitor resolution (1280x1024)

- An Internet account and connection (for Auto Update and export to YouTube)

* Additional disk resources are required when exporting projects.

For use with non-HD video and HD video (proxy support):

- Intel® Pentium® 4 Hyper-Threaded processor or AMD Athlon™ XP processor

For use with HD video (optional proxy support):

- Intel® Pentium® 4 Hyper-Threaded processor or Dual-core processor

- Fast hard disk (≥7200rpm drive)

For use with Full HD video (native AVCHD 1080):

- Quad-core processor

- 2GB RAM

Input device support

- FireWire® (IEEE1394) support for connecting tape-based camcorders

- USB support for file-based camcorders

- Video capture card for digitizing and editing analogue video clips

Output device support (for disc creation)

- CD-R Writer (for VCD)

- DVD±R (for DVD and AVCHD)

- Blu-Ray™ Disc Writer

Optional

- Windows XP Service Pack 2 (for HDV video capture)

First-time install

To install Serif MoviePlus X5, simply insert the disk into your computer's drive. The AutoRun feature automatically starts the Setup process. Just answer the on-screen questions to install the program.

Re-install

To re-install the software or to change the installation at a later date, select **Settings/Control Panel** from the Windows Start menu and then click on the **Add/Remove Programs** icon. Make sure the MoviePlus X5 disc is inserted into your drive, click the **Install...** button and then simply follow the on-screen instructions.

2 Getting Started

Startup Wizard

Once MoviePlus has been installed, you're ready to start. Setup adds a **Serif MoviePlus X5** item to the **All Programs** submenu of the Windows **Start** menu.

- Use the Windows **Start** button to start MoviePlus (or if MoviePlus is already running, choose **New>New from Startup Wizard...** from the **File** menu) to display the Startup Wizard.

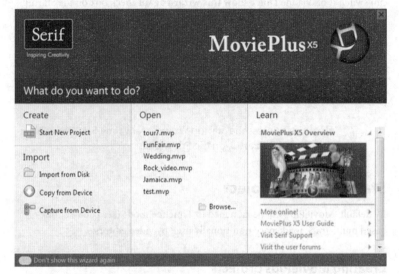

The Startup Wizard offers different routes into the program for you to explore:

- **Start New Project**, to create a new project based on SD or HD project settings.

- **Import from Disk***, to add media files from your **local disk** or **network drive** to a new project.

- **Copy from Device***, to copy and add media files from your file-based camcorder or removable device.

- **Capture from Device**, to capture video footage from your tape-based camcorder or analog device.

- **Open**, to quickly access previously saved or opened MoviePlus projects.

- **Learn**, to access online tutorials and more resources.

* Project settings are matched to your media file's format.

The Startup Wizard is displayed by default when you launch MoviePlus. You can switch it off via the **Don't show this wizard again** check box on the Startup Wizard screen, or on again via **Startup Wizard** in **Tools>Options...** (use the General menu option).

Click the **Cancel** button or press **Escape** on your keyboard to bypass the Startup Wizard and launch MoviePlus with an empty project. The type of project will match the last project you selected.

> You can also access the Startup Wizard at any time from **New>New from Startup Wizard...** on the **File** menu.

Starting a new project

By default, MoviePlus will be launched in Timeline mode (see p. 65), a time-based multi-track workspace traditionally used by video editors.

Creating MoviePlus projects

MoviePlus bases its movie compositions around "projects". A MoviePlus project file is a collection of project settings (the video size and shape, audio properties, aspect ratio, etc.) plus information about how all your clips are arranged and edited on the timeline.

The Startup Wizard lets you create projects either:

- without adding media files, as a blank project.

   OR

- based on your imported or copied media (e.g., from your camcorder), with media present in your Media pane.

To create a new project without adding media files:

- From the Startup Wizard, choose **Start New Project**.

  On first use, your project is based on PAL DVD project settings. For subsequent sessions, MoviePlus will remember and use the project settings used in the previous session.

  The blank project is now ready to have media files added to it (see p. 25).

 You can quickly check your project settings from the Status Bar, or, in more detail, via **File>Project Settings...**.

If you want to add media files immediately, you can base your project on your media file's source format. For example, as you add HD media files, your project will intelligently use HD project settings matching those specific media files. Your project is then set up with media files already present.

To create a new project that matches your media files:

1. From the Startup Wizard, choose:

   - **Import from Disk**. Locate and select your media files, then click **Open**.

     OR

   - **Copy from Device**. Using a wizard, choose your target device (e.g., camcorder), select files, then click **Finish**.

2. From the dialog, click **Yes** to change project settings to match the media file's source format. Click **No** to retain the project settings used in the previous session (ignoring the media file's format). Check **Don't ask me again** if you don't want to be prompted in future.

See Adding media files to your project (p. 25) for more information.

 In timeline mode, you can base your project on a clip's source format at any time by right-clicking a video or audio clip and choosing **Set Project Settings from Clip**.

As your project settings will be matched to your imported/copied media file, your export settings will also be matched to those modified project settings. As a result, choosing complicated project settings when starting your project and exporting is not required.

Creating custom project settings

You can customize your current project settings at any time by modifying its template.

To customize project settings:

1. Select **Project Settings...** from the **File** menu.

2. From the **Project Settings** dialog, pick a template in the **Templates** list on which to base your new project settings (or select the Multimedia preset for general use).

3. Click the **Modify** button to make a copy of the project, now named (**Untitled**).

4. Change various settings including the pixel size of your project, the **Pixel aspect ratio** (many types of output use stretched pixels), the video **Frame rate** (number of frames per second), **Interlacing**, and **Audio sampling rate**.

5. When you are happy with your settings you can save your project template for reuse—simply click the **Save** button, type a new preset name and click **OK**.

Opening an existing project

You can open an existing MoviePlus project from the Startup Wizard, **Standard** toolbar or the **File** menu.

To open a recently opened or saved project (via Startup Wizard):

1. From the Startup Wizard (at startup time or via **File>New...**), select your project from the **Open** section. The most recently opened or saved project will be shown at the top of the list.

    Open

    tour7.mvp
    tour2.mvp
    Rock_video.mvp
    FunFair.mvp
    Wedding.mvp
    Jamaica.mvp
    audio effects.mvp

2. Click the project name to open it.

 Recently viewed projects also appear at the bottom of the **File** menu. Simply select the file name to open it.

To open any project:

1. From the Startup Wizard (at startup time or via **File>New...**), click **Browse....**

   -or-

   Click 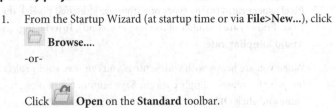 **Open** on the **Standard** toolbar.

   -or-

   Choose **Open...** from the **File** menu.

2. In the Open dialog, navigate to, then select the project name and click the **Open** button.

   You can also open projects by file drag-and-drop from Windows Explorer onto the MoviePlus workspace.

Adding media files to your project

The media files you use for your project could reside on a variety of devices, typically on your camcorder's hard disk or flash card/drive, but also on your mobile phone, digital camera, or computer drive (local, network, or removable disc).

You can add media files from these location as you start a new project (p. 21) or at any time by downloading, importing, capturing, or "ripping" media files into MoviePlus's Media pane.

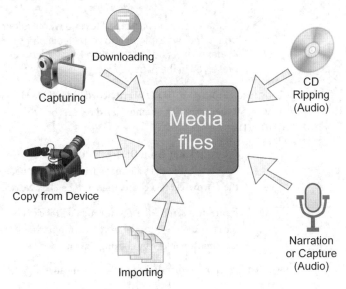

Media files are added by choosing an option from the ⊕ **Import Media** button on the **Tasks** toolbar or from the top of the Media pane. The drop-down list lets you:

Import	A standard dialog lets you navigate to, then select one or more media files from your **local disk** or **network drive** for import directly into your Media pane. Use **Shift**-select or **Ctrl**-select for adjacent or non-adjacent multiple selection before download. 🔍 You can also drag and drop files and whole folders from Windows Explorer into your Media pane. Folder names and any associated subfolders are preserved in the pane.
Copy from Device	Copy media from your **HD/DVD camcorder**, **USB Hard drive**, **USB memory stick**, **memory card reader**, or **CD/DVD**. • From the **Copy from Device** button, select the connected **Device** as a remote drive in the dialog, then **Browse...** to a chosen folder, then click **Next>**. • In the next screen, the device's media files can be selected and downloaded to your computer's **Destination** folder by clicking **Finish**. Selected files show in the Media pane automatically.
Capture	With your tape-based camcorder connected via USB/FireWire you can capture your movie's video footage and/or audio to a file, with optional scene detection.
Rip CD	Rip audio tracks from your favourite audio CDs straight into the Media pane.

The Media pane

The main purpose of the Media pane is to manage your media files before committing media to your storyboard or timeline.

You can perform several important operations from the pane.

- You can reorder files by clicking and dragging thumbnails into the position you wish them to appear on the storyboard (or timeline).

- You can fix incorrectly oriented images or movies obtained from your digital camera by using the **Rotate Left** and **Rotate Right** buttons.

- Trimming (p. 32) can be carried out by using   **Trim**.

Media files can then be added to your storyboard or timeline by drag and drop (see p. 47 and p. 72, respectively).

Remember that MoviePlus does not rotate or trim your original media, but instead on project "copies" of the original, thus preserving your valuable original media in their original file locations. Thumbnails in the Media pane are just links to their original files (try right-click **Properties...** to view file location). As a result, changes made to files within MoviePlus will not affect the originals.

Until now, we've just been using the Project tab. Two other tabs, **Library** and **Explorer**, are also available in the Media pane. The former stores media files for future use while the latter provides a "window" to your computer's folders and files—you can use media files directly from here but you won't be able to manage your files as you can in the Projects tab. See MoviePlus Help for more details.

Capturing video

MoviePlus makes it easy to **capture** your own video and audio footage to your PC from tape-based digital camcorders (e.g., Mini DV), analogue video sources (e.g., analogue camcorders, VHS, or TV; all via a capture card) or USB web cams.

Remember that videos stored on modern tapeless camcorders can be downloaded directly from the device's hard disk, flash card, or internal DVD. See Adding media files to your project on p. 25.

To set up and initiate the video capture, a Capture Video dialog is used.

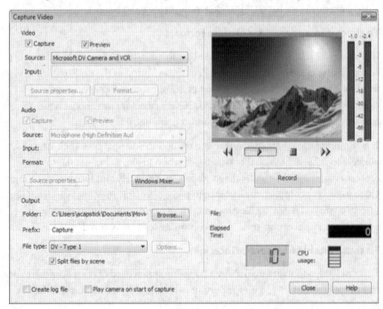

This example shows in-progress capture of digital video footage with associated audio from a tape-based camcorder. As you capture (by pressing the **Record** button), the footage is written to a file(s), which shows directly within the Media pane.

To begin capture:

1. Click the ⊕ **Import media** button on the **Tasks** toolbar (or Media pane).

2. From the drop-down list, select **Capture**.

To connect your camcorder or other capture device:

If your camcorder is properly connected and supported (and is set to playback mode rather than record mode if appropriate), you should see a video preview in the preview window of the Capture Video dialog when your camcorder is playing.

If you are using an analogue video source, ensure that it is connected to your video capture device (or a USB socket in the case of a web cam).

To choose an appropriate capture format:

If your source footage is on a tape-based camcorder, the video and audio capture settings are greyed out in the **Source Properties** button as the capture format is fixed to the camcorder's format. However, if your source footage is being captured via a video capture device or USB web cam, you can choose a file format suited to your video type by choosing this button.

It is recommended that you capture at a resolution and quality as high as possible to achieve high quality results—it is best to aim as high as the source footage resolution and quality. Even when you ultimately aim for your resulting video to be very compact, for instance to make it suitable for download from the Internet, you can defer the file-size-smashing resizing and compression operations to final export time, don't compromise your captured quality!

To set a suitable file storage location:

Captured video footage can occupy a large amount of hard drive space when it is transferred to your PC, so it is important to choose a drive location with lots of room.

- Choose **Options>Folders** from the **Tools** menu, then **Browse...** for a different **Capture** folder.

> During capture, you can define a different destination **Folder** within the Capture Video dialog (Output section).

To preview and cue your video footage:

For tape-based camcorders, transport controls under the preview window allow you to cue your tape to the point at which you would like capture to start; for other sources you'll need to control the device yourself, a remote control may be handy here.

To capture with scene splitting:

For DV video, the **Split files by scene** check box offers the chance for all your scenes to be saved as separate video files as part of the capture process. For capture from tape-based camcorder, the default is for the box to be checked so that scenes are split (by timestamp) where the recording has been stopped and restarted. For all other captures, if the box is unchecked, no splitting occurs so you'll capture a single video file.

For non-DV video, e.g. from analogue devices, scene splitting is not possible; the option is unavailable (greyed out) as time stamps are not present. Instead, scene detection can be carried out (see MoviePlus Help). Scene detection does not create separate video files but creates "virtual" scenes from a single video file.

> For HD video, scene splitting may not be possible—if so, the **Split file by scene** button will be greyed out.

Record

> Ensure that Video and Audio **Capture** check boxes in the Capture Video dialog are checked if you want to capture both audio and video. Check that your audio levels meter indicates that audio is being played.

1. Play your video source from at least a couple of seconds before the point at which you'd like capture to start (to allow the video device to begin playing smoothly), then press the [▶] button.

2. Click **Record** in this dialog to begin the capture.

3. To skip footage, press **Stop** to finish capture, then pause the playback by clicking the [▶"] button, cue the tape to the point you would like to proceed from, then play and record again to resume the capture.

> Don't use the "navigation" playback controls while recording!

> It's better to capture too much footage rather than too little, it can always be trimmed later, so don't worry too much about exactly how much is captured if you are uncertain.

4. When you are happy that all the required footage has been captured, click the **Stop** button, then the **Close** button.

> The captured video footage will show in your Media pane (see p. 27) automatically on closing the Capture Video dialog. The files are still physically located in your Capture Folder.

When MoviePlus captures your video or audio footage with scene detection, it will automatically name and incrementally number your files if you do not specify a particular filename (by default the Prefix "Capture" is used; the number is added as a suffix). To change the prefix name, enter a new name in the dialog's **Prefix** option.

Trimming

With audio or video clips, both duration and playback speed come into play. Most often, you'll want to shorten a clip without altering its playback speed— this is called **trimming**. For example, media files seldom begin or end exactly where you'd like; there may be extra frames at the beginning or end, or you may want to use a short section from the middle of the file. The solution is to trim the media file—adjusting its start and end point, called "in" and "out" points, to include just the section of video you want.

For any clip you can **split** your clip up into separate scenes, with each scene capable of being edited as for any other clip.

Clips can be trimmed or split in either your Media pane, or via the Storyboard or Timeline, by using the Trim dialog. Direct timeline trimming is also possible.

(A) Frame Preview, *(B)* Clip timeline, *(C)* Discarded end frames, *(D)* Out point, *(E)* Set In/Out Point, *(F)* Split, *(G)* Trim mode, *(H)* Playback controls, *(I)* Display controls: Show/Hide Video, Show/Hide Audio, Undo/Redo, Delete Scene, Zoom Out/In, *(J)* In point, *(K)* Discarded start frames.

To trim a single clip:

1. In the Media pane, select a clip and click 🖉 **Trim**.

    OR

    Select a video clip on the storyboard (or timeline) and click 🖉 **Trim** on the context toolbar.

2.   From the **Trim** dialog, to trim to a specific time/frame (using the
     Frame Preview):

   1.   Click on the ruler and drag the time indicator to the frame where
        you wish to trim before (or after), or use the playback controls for
        accurate frame-by-frame navigation.

   2.   Click the ⟦ **Set In Point** (or ⟧ **Set Out Point** button (or
        use the keyboard shortcuts **I** or **O**, respectively). The unwanted
        portion of the clip will appear in grey shading; the portion to be
        kept is highlighted in orange.

        Or, for trimming visually by frame:

        •   Hover your mouse cursor over the furthest left (or right)
            edge of the clip's timeline so that it changes to the **Trim**
            cursor, then drag the mouse to the right (or left) to trim
            away the start (or end) of your clip.

3.   Click the **OK** button.

You can move the **Slip** handle to shift the in/out points of a
trimmed clip at the same time. This "sliding window" lets you
change the content of the trimmed clip without changing its
duration.

Multi-trimming and splitting

MoviePlus lets you create multiple trimmed clips, called **scenes**, from a single
video clip. You may want to do this to remove unwanted footage within your
clip, e.g. removal of poorly recorded frames, or simply just to create more
manageable **scenes** for flexible video editing.

Multi-trimming simply involves either the creation of multiple in/out points or
splitting your clip; both methods let you define a new scene equally. Splitting on
its own does not remove content (like trimming) but instead just chops the clip
up.

°To apply multi-trimming:

1. From the Scenes dialog, click **Multi-trim**.

2. [   ]   Set the time indicator position successively for every in and
   out point, clicking **Set In Point** then **Set Out Point** (or use the
   keyboard shortcuts **I** or **O**, respectively) in turn as you move along the
   timeline. Unwanted portions of your clip will appear in grey shading;
   the portions to be kept appear as scenes in the dialog's right-hand
   pane. The orange portion indicates current selection.

Newly created scenes are added to your Media pane's Project tab (under a Scenes
folder). They can then be added to your Storyboard or Timeline.

To split your clip:

1. Display the Trim dialog as described previously, then click the **Multi-
   trim** button.

2. At the time indicator's position, click the   **Split** button (or use the
   keyboard shortcuts **S**). You'll see a new scene being created in the
   dialog's right-hand pane.

3. Repeat for creating multiple split clips.

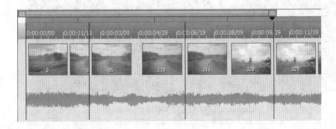

The thin black vertical lines indicate the split positions (there are three splits in the above example, creating four separate scenes).

Scene detection

For captured DV video not split at capture or captured analogue footage, you can perform scene detection via the Trim dialog—simply enable **Scene Detection** to create your virtual scenes. For more information, see MoviePlus Help.

Previewing your project

The Video Preview pane will help you check that your movie editing is going according to plan... you can preview your project at any time; MoviePlus will begin playing your video, will compose a realistic end result from the contents of your all video tracks, and will incorporate all transitions, effects, and other envelopes on the fly. Audio levels can be checked at the same time.

You can even continue editing your project while the preview is playing as your edits will be incorporated into the preview in real-time.

The lower **playback controls** operate much like your DVD player controls and allow you to navigate around your project during preview.

Go to Start

Jumps to the start of your project.

Previous Frame

Jumps to the previous frame in your project.

Click the **Play** or **Pause** button to start and pause the video preview, respectively. On play, the preview will begin from the current preview marker's position.

 Press the Space bar to play and pause.

Click the **Stop** button (or ESC key) to stop your video preview and reset the preview back to where it originally started.

Next Frame

Jumps to the next frame in your project.

Go to End

Jumps to the end of your project.

Shuttle

Allows you to vary the preview playback speed and direction by dragging from the centre point to the left (to reverse) or to the right (to fast forward); release the mouse to snap back to normal play speed. This is known as "trick play".

Additional buttons at the bottom of the pane offer previewing and editing options.

Select Tool

Lets you select objects (text, images, and shapes) in the pane for editing.

Pan Tool

Lets you drag an area of your video around the pane. When used with the right-click **Zoom in** option, this allows for more detailed analysis of your project.

Transform Tool

(only shown for a transform envelope in Timeline mode) The Transform button switches on the transform region to let you adjust your transform positioning.

Add Text

The **Add Text** button can be used to add either one or more text objects onto the currently selected clip or a new text clip (when clips are not selected). (See Adding text on p. 169).

Add Image

The button is used to add an image object to your text clip. This could be a saved frame (see below).

Add QuickShape

A QuickShape object can be created on your text clip within this pane.

Guides and Borders

From the flyout, switch on/off layout guide lines and TV-safe border.

Save/Copy Frame

The flyout allows the currently displayed frame to either be saved to an image file (use **Save Frame...**) or copied to the Clipboard (**Copy Frame**); the image can then be pasted as a graphic into a photo editing program, e.g. Serif PhotoPlus. Saving a frame adds the created image to your Media pane (Project tab).

Previewing in full screen

At some stage you may want to view your project in full screen view. As well as being able to see how your movie looks on a larger scale you'll be able view your project without guides and make use of dual monitors (one set at default size and one set as full screen).

To view in full screen:

- Click 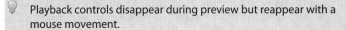 **Full Screen** on the **Tasks** toolbar.

> Playback controls disappear during preview but reappear with a mouse movement.

To close full screen view:

- Click ❌ **Close** to exit from full screen view.

Dual-monitor use

With dual monitors you can instantly preview your changes as you perform video editing. If you're a dual-monitor MoviePlus user, you can display your full screen view on your secondary monitor easily.

To operate dual monitors:

1. In full screen preview, click the 🖥️▾ button.

2. From the drop-down list, enable the "Monitor x" option from the drop-down list (where x is the secondary monitor number).

After closing full screen preview, the setting is remembered. The secondary monitor will automatically be used again for full screen preview.

- If you're experiencing poor playback performance (e.g., stuttering) you can:

  - Reduce the **Render Quality** (**Preview** menu).

  - Use pre-rendering.

- (For HD video), use proxy files in conjunction with pre-rendering when using computers that do not possess a quad-core processor.

Consult the Performance notes (p. 207) for more information.

3 Editing in Storyboard mode

Storyboard basics

 If you're in Timeline mode, click **Storyboard** to switch to Storyboard mode.

Storyboard mode provides the user with a simplified approach to movie making. If you're a beginner to video editing or you've no requirement for more complex multi-track editing techniques, the **storyboard** offers an easy-to-use workspace to build up your project and visualize different scenes in your movie. The easy-to-use storyboard is particularly suited to creating simple photo slideshows or movies containing a mixture of image and video clips.

A major strength of the Storyboard mode is its simplicity. You'll only see options, buttons, and dialogs that are needed for simple projects with the more advanced multi-video-track editing controls being hidden in another mode, called the Timeline mode (see p. 65). Think of the Storyboard and Timeline modes as being like two sides of a coin—you can flip between modes to jump between basic and advanced use any time you like.

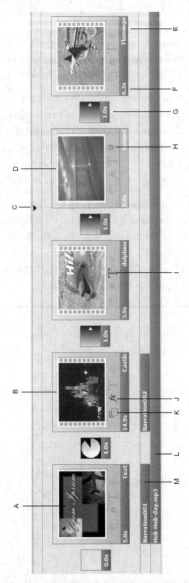

(**A**) Text clip, (**B**) Video clip, (**C**) Time indicator, (**D**) Image clip, (**E**) Clip name, (**F**) Duration, (**G**) Transition, (**H**) Chapter point, (**I**) Caption, (**J**) Effect(s), (**K**) Pan & Zoom, (**L**) Audio clip, (**M**) Audio clip (Narration).

Text clip

A text clip can be added for use as a static or rolling title or as credits. The clip has its own duration, and can be treated in a similar way to video/image clips. Additional text, as separate text objects, can be added onto the clip as captions. See Adding text on p. 169 for more information.

Video and image clips

Video and image clip thumbnails, representing your media elements, appear on the storyboard when added by drag-and-drop from the Media pane.

Time indicator

In storyboard mode, the time indicator is used to carry out a preview playback of your project from that point. The time indicator is also shown in the Video Preview pane for the same purpose.

Clip name

The clip name is the name of your media file by default. If required, you can edit the name in the Properties pane while the clip is selected.

Duration

The duration is the time the clip or transition will be displayed on screen. Video clip durations cannot be edited, but for text clips, image clips and transitions, click under their thumbnails to edit their values.

Transition

A cross-fade transition with a set duration is added between clips by default. The default transition can be swapped for another and have its duration altered. See Applying transitions on p. 52 for more information.

Chapter point

The   icon indicates that a marker, used exclusively when creating menus for your disc (DVD, Blu-ray, VCD), is associated with the clip. Your disc menu will include your chosen clip as a chapter, which can be clicked to play from that point in your movie. See Editing chapter properties on p. 194 for more information.

Caption

Static or animated captions can be added to any clip. They are superimposed onto the clip and, like text clips, can adopt a preset text style or be customized. Caption text can appear for the clip's duration or for a shorter time.

Effects

The ![fx] **Effects** icon indicates that an effect has been applied to the clip. Click the icon to view currently applied effects in the Properties pane (Effects tab). See Applying effects on p.136 for more information.

Pan & Zoom

The ![icon] **Pan & Zoom** icon indicates that a Pan & Zoom effect has been applied to the clip. Click the icon to view the current effect in the **Pan and Zoom** dialog. See Using Pan and Zoom on p.55 for more information.

Audio clips and Narration clips

A narration clip is added to a narration strip under your video or image clips after recording from a microphone. Likewise, audio clips show on their own Music strip that lies below the narration strip. Use both in combination for commentary over background music (e.g., soundtracks).

Adding media files

Media files show in your Media pane after capture, download or import (see Adding media files to your project on p. 25). Once present, it's a great idea to arrange the order of the files prior to adding them to the storyboard (see p. 47). This avoids having to rearrange clips in bulk on your storyboard itself. Once you're happy with the order you can add the media to the storyboard.

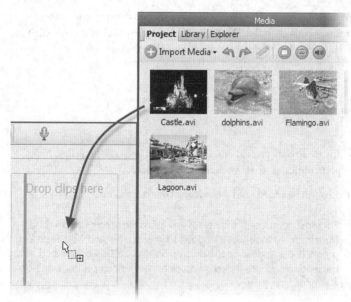

To add media to the storyboard:

1. From the Media pane, select your media, either:

   • Click to select a single media file.
     OR

   • For multiple media files:

     Use marquee select (to lasso files under a selection region).
     OR
     Use **Shift** key and click (to select a range of adjacent files).
     OR
     Use **Ctrl** key and click (to select a range of non-adjacent files).
     OR
     press **Ctrl+A** (to select all files).

2. Drag selected media onto your storyboard.

If the storyboard is empty, drag your clips directly into the empty workspace. Video or image clips go to the "Drop clips here" target areas, while audio clips snap onto horizontal narration or audio strips below the thumbnails.

If video clips are already present, insert your clip between existing clips. An insertion point indicates where your clip is to be placed.

Multiple clips will be added one by one along your storyboard.

 For most computers, MoviePlus will generate **proxy files** (p. 210) from your HD media as it's added to your storyboard. You'll see a progress bar appear on the bottom Status bar. This is expected behaviour, and aids video playback on slower computers. Don't be alarmed!

Selecting clips

When you are editing your movie and have already added a range of media clips to your storyboard, all your editing operations (including moves, trims, properties changes and other adjustments) are carried out on the selected clip. Clip selection is straightforward but several options can be used for multiple selection.

To select a single clip:

- Click on the clip. The clip's lower title bar turns orange.

To select multiple clips:

- Use **Shift** key and click (to select a range of adjacent clips).
  OR

- Use **Ctrl** key and click (to select a range of non-adjacent clips).
  OR

- Click **Select all clips** from the **Edit** menu (or press **Ctrl+A**).

When selected, the clip's thumbnail will show an orange bar underneath it to show that it is currently selected.

Arranging clips

The storyboard is a workspace that arranges clips automatically as they are dragged to the storyboard. When you first add clips to the Storyboard from the Media pane. the storyboard clip order is the same as the clip order in the Media pane. It therefore makes sense to arrange your clips in the Media pane first. As such there may not be a necessity to rearrange clips if the clip order is as intended. Realistically, it's often the case that you may want to further modify the clip order.

Once on the storyboard, an individual clip can be moved by drag and drop. The vertical marker indicates the target location for the moved clip.

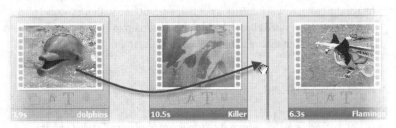

You can also copy and paste a clip by using options from the **Edit** menu. Both methods can also be carried out on multiple clips simultaneously.

Deleting clips

- To remove a clip, select it and press the **Delete** key. By multiple selection, you can remove more than one clip at the same time. Use **Ctrl**-click to select non-adjacent clips, **Shift**-click for adjacent multiple clips.

Resizing clips

If your added video or image clips are a different size and shape to your project settings, MoviePlus will not resize your media to fit the project size, leaving "black" bars (letterboxing) showing in the available space. Although you see black, the letterboxing is actually transparent (you're really seeing the default project background showing through).

The shape of the video in the Video Preview pane is determined by your project settings; if your clip properties and your project settings are different, you can decide what to do about the variance, i.e. you can leave the media with letterboxing or correct it via cropping.

Cropping removes unwanted borders either automatically by fitting to the Video Preview pane or by defining a crop area you draw yourself (anything outside the area is discarded); the clip is resized to fit the project. While used frequently on image clips (of unusual dimensions or if in Portrait orientation), you can also apply cropping to video clips—although it's important to ensure items of interest are not cropped out throughout the video clip's duration.

To resize a clip:

1. Select the clip.

2. Click **Fit** from the Storyboard toolbar and pick a resizing option from the drop-down list.

Letterbox - This is not normally set manually but can be used to override auto-cropping if this is deemed too excessive an action (if the clip's edges need to be preserved rather than removed by cropping).

Crop - This crops the clip to make it fit with the project size thus removing any letterboxing. The clip's aspect ratio is maintained so that the taller (or wider) areas are left outside the visible part of the project. See Cropping on p. 88 for more information.

Stretch - Stretches your clip horizontally or vertically to match the project video size—removing the letterboxing effect, but changing the clip's aspect ratio.

Custom - Launches the **Crop** dialog that lets you remove everything outside a defined crop area. Size the crop area by moving corner (maintaining aspect ratio) or side handles (alters aspect ratio) then position the crop area again by dragging; the clip will resize to fit the crop area. Click **Match project aspect** to set the crop area to the project aspect ratio.

 You can double-click on the crop area to reset its size back to the project's dimensions.

Applying transitions (storyboard)

MoviePlus supports many different transition types. For example, you can dissolve (**Cross-Fade**) between one clip and the next, or apply a variety of patterned wipes that use a moving edge or outline. Transitions such as **Iris Wipe**, **Cross-Blur** and **Zoom & Spin** are very popular in movie editing and are, of course, fully supported. MoviePlus can also produce some awe-inspiring 3D transitions—choose from 3D blinds, 3D Swap, 3D Flip, 3D Tumble, 3D Page Roll, to name but a few.

Transitions are displayed as inter-clip thumbnails in Storyboard mode, which change according to transition applied (the thumbnail represents the transition's function). The transition's duration is shown under its thumbnail. Some examples include:

Cross-fade   *3D*   *Blinds*
(default)   *Page Roll*   *feathered*

Each transition is applied to the start of a clip—this is called an In transition.

You may notice a zero-length "transition" at the start and end of your storyboard.

This is a straight cut, but you can create **fade ins** or **fade outs** from/to black by changing the transition duration from 0.0s.

To change a transition's duration:

- Click the duration time under the transition thumbnail, enter a new value, then press the **Enter** key.

Changing this value will automatically "ripple" all other subsequent clips along the storyboard with respect to time.

To replace a transition:

1. Select one or more transitions on the storyboard. For multiple transitions, **Ctrl**-click on each transition one-by-one; for all transitions, right-click any transition, and select **Select all transitions**.

2. Click **Transition Gallery** on the context toolbar.

3. From the dialog, choose a category from the upper window. In the lower window, review the presets available (their names indicate their intended function). Select a preset, e.g. 3D Page Roll.

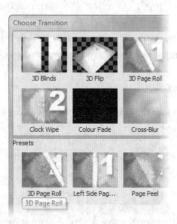

4. Click **OK**.

💡 For a quick way to replace transitions, open the Galleries pane, select the **Transitions** tab, then drag and drop a transition thumbnail onto your transition.

💡 Hover over any preset to see a preview of how your transition will look!

To modify a transition:

1. Select the transition thumbnail.

2. From the transition's Properties pane, alter the transition's properties at the bottom of the pane.

To delete a transition:

• Simply select a transition and press the **Delete** key.

The result is simply a cut: in less than the blink of an eye, the last frame of the first clip is replaced by the first frame of a second clip. To reinstate the transition at a later date, enter a transition value other than 0.0s.

To save a modified transition to a new name:

- Click 🖫 **Add to Gallery** at the top of the Properties pane. Once named, the transition appears as a new preset in the appropriate folder in the Choose Transition dialog (or Transitions tab in the Galleries pane).

Using pan and zoom

Pan and zoom "Ken Burns" effects can be used on any clip, but the effect really comes into its own when used on image clips. Rather than displaying clips that always display at the same size, you can easily apply panning and zooming effects that create variety and interest in your project.

The effect is applied by using a dual-pane dialog, the left-hand **Start** pane
representing the start of the clip and the right-hand **End** pane, the end of the
clip. Simply adjusting the resizable selection area in each pane sets the zoom
level or pan position.

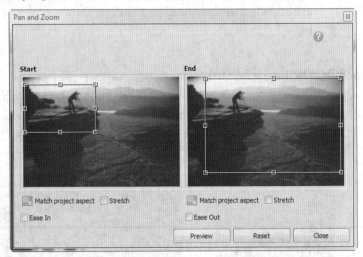

To pan and zoom your clip:

1. Click the clip on the storyboard (or timeline).

2. Select **Pan & Zoom** on the context toolbar.

3. From the dialog's **Start** pane, drag a corner or edge control handle (for
    maintaining aspect ratio or unconstrained sizing) on the selection
    area. Use the **Alt** key to resize the area in relation to the centre of the
    area (rather than the opposite corner or edge). Once sized, reposition
    the area with the hand cursor. If needed, click the **Reset** button to reset
    each selection area back to the default size.

4. Adjust the area on the End pane in a similar way.

5. (Optional) Click **Match project aspect** on either pane to make the
    aspect ratio of that pane's selection area match that of your project.

6. (Optional) Check **Ease In** or **Ease Out** on respective panes to apply a non-linear rate of change to your pan and zoom (Quadratic slow interpolation).

7. Click **Close** to save your resized or repositioned areas.

The result is two sized areas which, on playback, MoviePlus will pan and zoom between according to the position and size of each area, respectively.

Using CG clips

Several types of Computer Generated (CG) clips exist within MoviePlus. They differ from video or audio clips in that they are not captured by camcorder, but are created from within MoviePlus itself. The following types of CG clip are available:

- **Backgrounds**
  To apply simple solid or gradient colours as a clip. Use to introduce colour either as part of a fade-in or fade-out or as a background to text. Other uses include recolourizing semi-opaque video clips and masking shapes or text over a background colour.

Solid Fill, Linear Gradient, Elliptical Fill, Conical Fill

- **QuickShapes**
  To add modifiable ready-made drawn shapes such as stars, hearts, spirals and many more. QuickShapes are great for techniques such as masking.

Star, Heart, Spiral

What CG clips all share is that they are managed in a very similar way within MoviePlus, i.e. they can have colour, transparency and effects applied to them.

To apply a CG clip:

1. In Storyboard mode, select a clip (the clip before which the CG clip will be added).
    OR
    On the timeline, position your time indicator on the timeline.

2. Select your chosen CG clip type from the **CG Clip>** option on the **Insert** menu. By default, a white background or a QuickShape Ellipse is added.

It's very likely that your CG clip will need to be modified, either to change its colour or transparency. For QuickShapes, you'll more than likely want to change the QuickShape type (see p. 61).

 You'll find some ready-to-go sample gradient backgrounds or QuickShapes in the Media pane (Library tab), under Samples>Fills or Samples>Quickshapes. Simply drag to your storyboard or timeline.

Adjusting a clip's colour

MoviePlus offers a number of ways to apply colour to CG clips in MoviePlus. You can apply solid or gradient colours to any clip's fill.

A new colour is selected from a spectrum of preset colours or from a Colour Picker (both accessible via the **Fill** button on the clip's Properties pane).

For gradient fills you can adjust the gradient path of any gradient fill and the colours used to make up the gradient (by clicking a square node and changing the colour).

Adjusting a clip's transparency

Transparency is great for highlights, shading and shadows, and simulating "rendered" realism. It can make a huge difference between your clips looking "flat" and appearing with depth and snap. MoviePlus fully supports variable transparency and lets you apply solid or gradient transparency to your CG clips.

Like fills, transparency can be applied from the clip's Properties pane. Select the **Transparency** button and choose a percentage **solid** transparency (via slider) or pick from a spectrum of preset **gradient** transparencies. If necessary, you can edit the transparency path.

- **Solid** transparency distributes the transparency evenly across the object.

- **Gradient** transparencies (Linear, Ellipse, and Conical), provide a simple gradient effect, with a range from clear to opaque.

Varying the transparency of a CG clip gives the effect of variable erasure, but it leaves the original object intact—you can always remove or alter the transparency later. Transparencies work rather like fills that use "disappearing ink" instead of colour. A gradient transparency varies from more "disappearing" to less, as in the hexagon above.

To save your CG clip:

- Change the clip's name, then click the  **Add to Media pane** at the top of the clip's Properties pane. The clip will appear in the Media pane's Project tab.

Fading with backgrounds

At the beginning or end of your project you can introduce a fade in or fade out by using a background clip. Such clips can be editable gradient fills (linear, ellipse and conical) as well as solid colours. They can equally be applied between clips to act as a coloured interlude (possibly with added captions).

- On the storyboard, using a fade in as an example, you can introduce a background clip before the initial clip (**Insert>CG Clip>Background**).

- On the timeline, you can do the same but ensure the time indicator is set to the start of your project. If the clip you want to fade in to is already at the left edge of your timeline, leaving no room for the background clip at the beginning of the timeline, you should move your video/image clip(s) further down the timeline, creating some room at the start of your project. If you've already created a complex composition with multiple clips and tracks—so moving the first clip would disrupt the rest of your project—MoviePlus can move all of your later clips at the same time when a clip is dragged. This automatic moving of clips is called Rippling (see MoviePlus Help).

Other timeline fading methods can be carried out using Colour-Fade or Cross-Fade transitions.

More about QuickShapes

You're more than likely to swap the default Ellipse for a different shape. An impressive selection of QuickShape types can be chosen from, and once you've picked a type, you can further morph its shape—all from within the QuickShape's Properties pane. The ability to further alter the appearance of any QuickShape type makes them more flexible and convenient than clipart pictures with similar designs.

To change your QuickShape type:

Once added to your timeline, the QuickShape type can be edited in its Properties pane (or by pressing **F4**). The lower portion of this pane hosts several options which will affect your QuickShape's appearance, i.e.

- Click the **QuickShape type** drop-down list to swap the default QuickShape Ellipse for your preferred shape.

- The QuickShape preview window updates to show the current QuickShape, without colour fills or effect applied. This lets you focus on the main purpose of the window—to morph your QuickShape with ease.

 The **Stretch to project size** checkbox, if checked, will ensure that the QuickShape will fully occupy the frame size.

To morph your QuickShape design:

- In the preview window, select a square control handle appearing next to the shape. Different QuickShapes have different handles. To find out what each handle does for a particular shape, move the control handles while reading the Status Bar. You can alter shapes dramatically with combinations of control handle adjustments. It's best to experiment!

4 Editing in
Timeline mode

Timeline basics

Introduction

 Click **Timeline** to switch from Storyboard to Timeline mode.

For more advanced projects (compared to simpler storyboard-driven projects), the timeline lets you organize all your video and audio footage on **multiple tracks**, sequence clips one after the other, add and edit envelopes, effects, and so much more. The timeline offers the equivalent of all the manual editing operations that traditional film editors need and it allows for post-production alterations.

The timeline has two basic dimensions, height and length. Horizontal length relates to the duration of your project: your timeline has markings along a ruler to indicate the passing of time, starting with zero at the left of the timeline. Any clips added to your timeline will follow a playback sequence from left to right. You can position the start point for previews (or the point at which you'd like to perform an edit) using a vertical marker called the **Time indicator**—this shows on both the timeline and as a preview marker in the Video Preview pane. The height of the timeline is related to the number of video or audio tracks used— you'll need to introduce more tracks if tackling advanced editing techniques including overlays, masking, blue/green-screening etc.

We'll describe some terminology used for various parts of the timeline and your project so that understanding timeline operations becomes clearer.

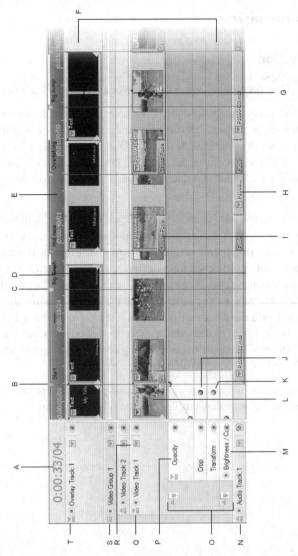

(**A**) Counter, (**B**) Chapter Point, (**C**) Marker, (**D**) Time Indicator, (**E**) Timeline ruler,
(**F**) Strips, (**G**) Video Clip, (**H**) Audio Clip, (**I**) Transition, (**J**) Selected Keyframe,
(**K**) Unselected keyframe, (**L**) Image Clip, (**M**) Effect, (**N**) Audio Track,
(**O**) Keyframe View, (**P**) Envelopes, (**Q**) Video Track, (**R**) Attributes menu button,
(**S**) Video Group, (**T**) Overlay Track.

Timeline elements

Headers

Headers control the strip they are attached to. In the case of tracks and groups, adjustments to the header can affect all the clips on a track or all the tracks in a group (or both), respectively. You can select the track/group by clicking its name, mute (and unmute) to disable or enable its contents in the project composition, and display envelopes for opacity and transform (for video tracks/groups) or volume and pan (for audio tracks or audio buses); a clip's crop envelope may also be shown along with its opacity and transform envelope. Track-wide effects may also be displayed.

The header may also show a clip's envelope or applied effects—these attributes are revealed by clicking its ☑ **Attributes** button, and selecting an attribute.

Strips

Strips are the horizontal "stripes" running the length of the timeline (to the right of the headers section) that can store your clips. Each strip allows you to edit and arrange clips, as well as edit their effects, transitions, and envelopes. Each strip is accompanied by a header to its left.

Video/Image/Audio Clip

A clip is a media element; an "object" you can place on a timeline track. Clips can also include Computer-Generated (CG) clips (backgrounds, text, and QuickShapes). It's important to appreciate the difference between clips, tracks and groups because MoviePlus will allow you to add effects, for instance, to each or all of them with differing results.

Video/Audio Track

A track is just a straightforward combination of a single strip and its header. You can add multiple clips to a track by dropping a multiple selection from the Media pane onto your track's strip. The clips will be added to the timeline in succession with a default overlap. You can apply effects and envelopes (like opacity or a transform) to tracks, which will have a resulting effect on all the clips on that track. MoviePlus supports multiple audio and video tracks so that it is possible to compose more complicated projects with "layers" of video using fades to reveal underlying layers.

A Music Track is also provided for optional soundtracks.

The Overlay Track, shown on a new project's timeline, is used to host text captions such as movie titles as well as video overlays. Titles will be superimposed over underlying movie content. These are dragged from the Galleries pane (Titles tab).

Video Groups

Groups are not only a way of keeping complex compositions tidy—you can also restrict editing to selected tracks by placing them inside a **Video Group**. Effect Groups, for both Video and Audio, work in an identical way for global effect control. The **View** menu also has an option to **Show Master Groups**, a top-level group to allow you to mute, apply effects to, or adjust envelopes for all video or all audio at once.

Keyframe View

When you add an envelope or effect to a clip, track, or group, or when you want to edit an existing envelope, effect or transition, the **Keyframe View** is displayed directly underneath the clip, track, or group.

Keyframes

Keyframes are points along a strip associated with a clip, track, or group's attributes (envelope, effect, or transition). The keyframe stores your chosen settings for use at a specific point of time along your timeline. Using more than one keyframe along a strip, MoviePlus automatically (and gradually) changes from one keyframe's settings to the next keyframe's settings as time passes between them. For example, on an opacity envelope, a keyframe at time zero with a setting of 0% opacity followed by another keyframe two seconds later with a setting of 100% would cause a gradual "fade in" effect over a period of two seconds. The keyframes can have their properties modified in the Properties pane when selected, and can be moved along the timeline to different points.

Envelopes, Effects and Transitions

Any time a clip, track, or group's keyframe View is displayed via a common Attributes menu (see p. 68), the strips that show belong to one or more attributes of that object. Each attribute can be of type envelope, effect, or transition, and are grouped together for easy management. Normally you'll see envelopes, effects or transitions, but not all three attribute types all at once (this saves valuable timeline space). Each clip, track, or group cannot possess more than one envelope of the same type; only two transitions can be set on any single clip (you can't set a transition on a track). There is no restriction on the number of effects a clip, track, or group can have.

Marker

Markers act as guides on your timeline to indicate key time location or events that occur within your project. They can be labelled, positioned and navigated equally.

Chapter point

A chapter point is a type of marker that is used exclusively for disc creation. Each chapter point placed on your timeline defines the start of your chapters shown in your disc menu.

Set Selection Start/End

Selection markers set a start and end range on your timeline within which any encompassed clips will be either pre-rendered (for optimized preview performance) and/or exported to file, PSP, or iTunes (Apple devices). The markers apply to all clips, tracks and groups down the entire height of the timeline. Limiting your export range is ideal for sharing only a chosen section of the movie, rather than the whole movie.

Time indicator

The time indicator, the blue vertical line you can see spanning the height of the timeline and its ruler, is most easily thought of as your editing marker. It allows you to set a precise position for splits and trims, allows clips and keyframes to be accurately positioned on your project timeline, and can be used along the timeline ruler to play back a preview of your project from that point. You can also position your time indicator over the start/end of a clip then single-click to set a precise time indicator position. The time indicator is also shown in the Video Preview pane to indicate your playback position during playback.

Timeline ruler

The ruler runs along the top of the timeline and shows you the current time range for the visible part of your project. You can zoom in or out of the timeline using a mouse wheel to display more or less of your project timeline on screen. A single-click on the ruler will position the time indicator marker for editing or video preview. You can alter your ruler units using the **View** menu's **Ruler Units** flyout. The default setting of "Time and Frames" is in the format *hh:mm:ss/ff*, representing hours, minutes, seconds and frames (of video), respectively.

Counter

The counter sits at the top-left of your timeline and shows you time at the time indicator. It uses the format set in the **View** menu's **Ruler Units** flyout.

Clip/track indicators and buttons

An LED in the top-left corner indicates if the clip (or track) is included in the composition (green) or if it is temporarily disabled (red). If you mute a track/group, the track/group header and each clip on that track/group would show a red LED to indicate that they are disabled. Clips also have blue triangular handles at each end that can be dragged to introduce an automatic cross fade (the fade can be replaced with a different transition by dragging and dropping a transition preset onto the clip's blue transition bar).

Attributes menu

On clips and track/group headers—clicking the ▼ **Attributes** button displays an **Attributes menu**, which is used to show envelopes, effects or transitions applied (along with their keyframes). The button will display in different colours according to selection and if the object's attributes have been modified, i.e.

   ▼ Grey/White. Attributes unselected and unmodified.

   ▼ Red/White. Attributes selected and unmodified.

   ▼ Grey/Yellow. Attributes unselected and modified.

   ▼ Red/Yellow. Attributes selected and modified.

Mute

Any clip, track or group can be muted at any time during video preview. You may want to temporarily switch off an audio track while you are editing and previewing the same track again and again. Equally, you may want to mute or "black out" a particular clip while testing your project.

👁 🎧 Muting is possible by clicking the respective **Mute** buttons on a video or audio track's header. For a video or audio clip, you can right-click and select the **Mute** option.

📌 To keep the attribute(s) on permanent display, click the drawing pin in the header of your clip, track or group's attributes strip. Click again to hide.

Adding and arranging tracks

In Timeline mode, three tracks are displayed on the timeline by default, i.e. the Overlay Track, Video Track, and Audio Track. The empty video and audio tracks will allow a video and its linked audio clip (if present) to be dragged onto each track from the Media pane.

 The empty Overlay track can take text (as captions) or video (for blended video overlays).

To add extra tracks:

- Choose **Video Track** or **Audio Track** from the **Insert** menu. The track is inserted directly above any selected track of the same type.

Use the **Shift** key as you insert to add a new track below any selected track rather than above it.

To change the track order:

- Drag the appropriate track header further up or down the stack of headers at the left of the timeline. You'll see a grey line between tracks and a place cursor where your track can be inserted. Release the mouse button to place.

The above example reorders two simple video tracks (selected Video Track 3 is dragged to be placed above Video Track 2).

Adding media files

Media files show in your Media pane after download, import, or capture (see Adding media files to your project on p. 25). Once present, it's a great idea to arrange the order of the files prior to adding them to the timeline (see below). This avoids having to rearrange clips in bulk on your timeline itself. Once you're happy with the order you can add the media to the timeline.

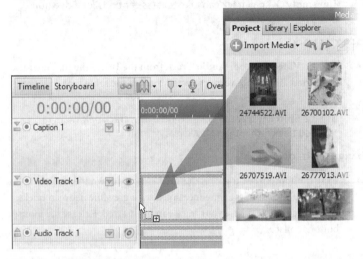

To add media to the timeline:

1. From the Media pane, select your media, either:

    ● Click to select a single media file.
    OR

    ● For multiple media files:

       Use marquee select (to lasso files under a selection region).
       OR
       Use **Shift** key and click (to select a range of adjacent files).
       OR
       Use **Ctrl** key and click (to select a range of non-adjacent files).
       OR
       press **Ctrl+A** (to select all files).

2. Drag selected media onto your timeline. Multiple clips will be added one by one along your timeline. Tracks suitable to specific clip types will be offered.

> Video and image clips must be located on video tracks, and of course audio on audio tracks.

> For most computers, MoviePlus will generate proxy files (p. 210) from your HD media as it's added to your timeline. You'll see a progress bar appear on the bottom Status bar. This is expected behaviour, and aids video playback on slower computers. Don't be alarmed!

Selecting clips (timeline only)

When you are editing your movie and have already added a range of media clips to your timeline, all your editing operations (including moves, trims, properties changes and other adjustments) are carried out on the selected object(s). So, let's cover how you go about selecting clips!

The good news is that you can simply click on clips to select them. Whether it's a video, image, audio, or text clip, a click will outline it in orange to show you that it is selected. Track or group names (in the header) also show in orange.

Clips obtained for your camcorder will have both a video and audio clip—you'll see each displayed next to each other on the timeline. Selection of the video clip, will always select the audio clip, and vice versa.

Selecting multiple clips

You can select multiple clips (including clips that are linked) as follows:

*   To select **non-adjacent** clips, hold the **Ctrl** key down on your keyboard and click each clip you would like to include in the selection. Ctrl+click again to remove a clip from the current selection.

*   To select **adjacent** clips on a single track, click a clip at one end of your proposed selection range, hold the **Shift** key down and click on the clip at the other end. All clips in between, plus the selected clips, are selected.

- For **marquee selection**, hold your primary mouse button down and drag a rectangle on your timeline—anything touching (and also anything inside) the rectangle will become selected.

When multiple clips are selected, you can perform stretching on all clips simultaneously.

To make your multiple selection a permanent feature of your timeline for continuous easy editing, you can create a Link as described in Arranging clips (see p. 79).

How selected objects are displayed

Object	Selection status
	Clip has been clicked and is selected (an orange border appears around the object). You can now modify its properties in the Properties pane, and perform other operations (trim, fit, etc). The linked audio clip below the video clip shows a blue border when the video clip is selected. When any object in a link is selected, all other items in the link take on this "blue" selection highlight. Although not actually selected, edits will affect it.
	Link overlays show in light blue.

This clip has had one of its envelopes, effects, or transitions modified (e.g., a keyframe below the tracks in the Keyframe View area) as the Attributes button has changed from grey/white to red/yellow.

(Grey) A keyframe on an envelope, effect, transition, background, QuickShape or text strip. This keyframe is not selected.

(Red) A keyframe selected by single-click. You can now modify this keyframe's properties via the attributes Properties pane.

A track is selected when its name is highlighted. Other strip headers (clip strip headers, effects/envelope/transition strip headers) have a similar appearance.

This track has had one of its envelopes, effects or transitions modified.

Zooming, scrolling, seeking, and scrubbing (timeline only)

To see more or less of your project at one time or to navigate your project, you can perform various operations along your timeline.

Zooming

The Timeline toolbar hosts a series of very useful tools for zooming your timeline.

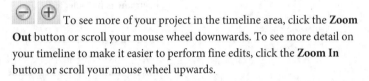 To see more of your project in the timeline area, click the **Zoom Out** button or scroll your mouse wheel downwards. To see more detail on your timeline to make it easier to perform fine edits, click the **Zoom In** button or scroll your mouse wheel upwards.

You can use the zoom slider on your timeline as an alternative to using the Zoom buttons.

To see your entire project within the available timeline area—simply click the **Zoom to All** button.

If your time indicator is out of view due to a zoom operation or playback of your project preview, select **Scroll to Time Indicator** from the View menu to jump to the time indicator's current position.

Scrolling

To scroll the timeline horizontally, hold down the **Shift** key while using your mouse wheel, or to scroll vertically, hold down the **Ctrl** key.

 It's also possible to drag your time indicator to the left or right edge of your window to scroll previously hidden parts of your timeline into view.

Seeking

The Video Preview pane also helps with some seek operations.

- The ▐◄ **Go to Start** and ►▌ **Go to End** buttons let you jump to the beginning or end of your project, respectively.

- ◄▌ ▐► For fine tuning the position of the time indicator (i.e., frame stepping or frame advance), for instance to perform a trim operation at a specific frame of video, you can use the **Previous Frame** and **Next Frame** buttons.

- The **Shuttle** control allows you to vary the preview playback speed and direction by dragging from the centre point to the left (to reverse) or to the right (to fast forward).

Your preview will update any time the time indicator is moved, so you should always use the preview in conjunction with your editing operations.

Scrubbing

Scrubbing might seem an unusual term but it is an extremely useful feature! You may already know that clicking along the ruler above the timeline sets your time indicator's position. However, if you click and drag along the ruler, MoviePlus will preview your project at the speed of the drag—as your mouse passes along the timeline in either direction, the preview will show you the current frame. This allows you to pass your mouse over an area of the timeline to preview a specific section without starting and stopping preview playback.

Arranging clips (timeline only)

Arranging clips on your timeline is crucial to building interesting, more complex projects—typically to create a rich multi-track multimedia project with the most popular video editing techniques.

Simple arrangement—clips following one another

When you want one clip—a video or image—to directly follow on from another clip, they need to touch each other on the timeline with no space in between them. When one "scene" follows another in this way, it's often referred to as a "cut" although you don't need to get the scissors out to achieve it with MoviePlus.

Simply drag clips along on the same track so that they are positioned next to each other. When two clips are close together the one you are dragging will snap into place.

 A default cross-fade transition shows between multiple clips when dragged onto the timeline.

Making one clip appear on top of another

MoviePlus uses multiple tracks in a similar fashion to the way photo-editors (such as Serif's own PhotoPlus) use multiple layers. Many compositions are perfectly fine with one "layer" but you can introduce some interesting effects by layering your images or videos on top of each other.

MoviePlus composes your video based on timeline content, working from the top downwards. If you have multiple tracks in your project with a full-size video on the top layer, it could well obscure all underlying tracks because you can't see through it... but if your top-most track (or clips on it) contains Images (with transparency), Background, QuickShape or Text clips with reduced opacity, resized video or images using a transform envelope, video with a mask applied or a Chroma Key effect, you will be able to see through to underlying tracks.

So, to make one clip an overlay appearing on top of other clips, add an additional video track (choose **Video Track** on the **Insert** menu), then place the video or image you would like to appear as an overlay on the top track. All tracks support images or video with transparency, and all tracks follow the same timeline, so objects are almost as easy to arrange when using multiple tracks as they are for single-track projects.

For caption text superimposed on underlying video, you can use the default Overlay Track which can take any Title caption presets dragged from the Galleries pane.

Deleting clips

Any selected clip on your timeline can be deleted by pressing the **Delete** key. Any accompanying linked clip will also be deleted, i.e. a video clip and its associated audio clip are removed simultaneously.

Linking clips together for easy editing

Automatically-linked clips

When you add a video clip to your timeline, you will normally find that two clips are added to your timeline—one video clip and one audio clip, on an adjacent video and audio track, respectively.

This is because the video file contained both an audio and video stream that MoviePlus has separated for you for editing purposes. Because these two streams came from the same location, MoviePlus automatically links them together. When clips are linked, edits to one of the objects will affect other linked objects. If you select your video clip and perform a split, for instance, the linked audio clip will split in the same place.

When moving clips, any linked clips on different tracks will move to new relative locations on the timeline providing there is enough space on each track for your clips to relocate to.

Temporarily disabling Linking

There are occasions where you may find the need to temporarily disable Linking, for instance when trying to trim clips that are part of a Link, discard an unwanted audio track (below), or copying a clip independently of its linked clips.

Unlinking/linking media

Linking operations can be carried out in several ways:

- By clicking 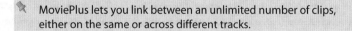 **Linking** on the Timeline context toolbar. Ensure clips are selected.

  OR

- Via right-click **Link and Group**> submenu (or via **Edit** menu).

  - Select **Unlink** to unlink the clips (or **Unlink All** to unlink all currently linked clips).

  - Select **Link** to establish a link between selected video and audio clip (if the clips are not already linked).

> MoviePlus lets you link between an unlimited number of clips, either on the same or across different tracks.

Unlinking/linking overlays

Link overlays are used to associate a video clip with an overlay, e.g. a caption such as a movie title or credits, superimposed over your video footage.

By their nature, overlays have to occupy a higher level video track **above** any given track. The overlay could equally be another video clip.

By linking, you can keep control of your overlays when moving your video clip, as the overlay will move with it. The overlay can be moved independently, but will always move with your video clip while linked.

Linking/unlinking operations are as described for Unlinking/Linking media described previously but by using equivalent **Link Overlay** and **Unlink Overlay** options instead.

 Linked overlays show with a light blue border when selecting the underlying video clip.

Grouping clips

The selection of multiple clips allows you to move those clips around your timeline at the same time, but only while they remain selected. As a more permanent solution for dragging, copying, and deleting, grouping clips makes a connection between clips until you choose to ungroup them. The grouped clips can be moved together at any time, until ungrouped.

Grouping operations described below are provided in a **Link and Group>** right-click menu, but are all also available from the **Edit** menu.

- **Group**: Groups two or more selected clips. If you've got grouped files already selected, use **Ctrl**-click to select another clip to be grouped, then select this option.

- **Ungroup**: Select a file already grouped, then choose this option to remove just the selected file from the group.

- **Ungroup All**: Click any grouped file then select this option to ungroup itself and all other files that are grouped.

Grouped clips show on your timeline with a dark-blue border; the selected clip, being part of the group, will show with an orange border.

 Groups are ignored when trimming—you'll be able to trim clips without affecting the grouping.

Aligning frames

The **Align To Frames** option on the **Arrange** menu will enable and disable snapping to the nearest frame of video. Video frames are typically about 30 or 40 milliseconds apart (there's typically 25 or 30 frames per second of video), so you can choose whether your Time indicator-based editing snaps to these divisions or is totally freeform. Frame snapping, or align to frames, is the normal mode to work with unless you are trimming audio to a very fine degree.

Rippling

Rippling is a design aid that takes some of the headache out of making room on your timeline, or taking up slack (empty) space on the timeline by keeping your clips' relative positions constant when you make edits (this also includes a clip's keyframes). Rippling saves you the effort of moving multiple clips for the sake of what is often a minor edit, perhaps to make room at the start of your project for titles or a new intro or the deletion of a section of video from the middle of a project. You can enable and disable Rippling using either the **Rippling** button on the timeline's context toolbar, or by using the command on the **Arrange** menu.

Moving clips

Rippling affects other clips (and their envelope, effect or transition's keyframes) starting at the same time or after the clip you are moving. When you move a clip, those other clips that start at the same point or later on the timeline will shuffle left or right to account for your move.

When trimming or extending the end of a clip

Rippling only affects other clips that both start after your edited clip starts and end after the end of your edited clip.

When trimming the start of a clip

Rippling affects other clips that start and end after the start of your edited clip, and it also moves your edited clip to the same "start time" it had before you trimmed its start, shuffling other affected clips at the same time.

Ripple mode

Rippling can be set to work in one of four modes: it can affect the track you are working on, all tracks of the same level (e.g., those within a group), all tracks on the same level including marker rippling, or the whole timeline (with marker rippling). The last two options allow markers to maintain their positions relative to the moved clips—otherwise marker positions will not alter when rippling takes place.

Rippling with complex projects

For complex multi-track projects, you might worry that Rippling won't manage all the necessary moves—don't worry, Rippling works regardless of the number and type of clips or tracks involved. Providing you have selected the appropriate **Ripple mode** you can move a large number of clips that span multiple tracks by having Rippling enabled. Be sure to select an appropriate timeline zoom level when selecting and moving your clips—you may wish to use a low zoom level (to see all of your project) to make the move easy, but you might find that using a higher zoom level (seeing just a few small clips) allows you to more easily select and drag the correct clip. MoviePlus will automatically scroll the timeline in the direction of your drag until you centre your mouse to choose a "drop zone", but you could instead type a new start time for your selected clip in the Properties pane—Rippling works however a clip is moved.

Snapping

Snapping is a design aid that helps you achieve neat layouts. When you are moving objects around on the timeline (or trimming/stretching them), snapping makes your edit jump to the nearest clip, to the position of the time indicator, to the beginning of the timeline, and to a default transition overlap value.

By default, snapping is enabled, although you can switch it off from the **Arrange** menu. To control which elements do and do not get snapped to, or to adjust snap sensitivity, visit the **Snapping** tab (**Tools>Options**). Hold down **Alt** during your editing operations to temporarily switch snapping off (or on, if disabled).

Using groups (timeline only)

Video groups

Video groups serve a couple of important functions on MoviePlus's timeline. Firstly, they can help keep related tracks together for easy management. For instance, applying an effect to a video group means that all tracks within the group inherit the effect.

Video Group 1 contains Video Track 1 and Video Track 2 (but not the Background Video track). The Adjust HSL effect has been applied to the Group (and therefore Tracks 1 and 2 simultaneously). Background Video is not subject to the effect.

The next main function for video groups is more complicated but very useful, i.e. limiting the range of a transparency effect or mask. Masks and the Chroma Key effect are both methods of achieving transparency (see p. 114 and 118).

To add a video group:

1. Select the video track above which you want to insert a group.

2. Choose **Video Group** from the **Insert** menu.

Once you've created a group you have to then associate chosen tracks to the group.

To add a track to a group:

- Drag and drop the track over the group header.

The track will be nested under the group if the operation is successful.

To drag a track out of a group, aim to drop the track at the bottom edge of the group or any header position that is as wide as the group's header.

If using video groups, click the ⬜ **Collapse/Expand** button to collapse the group's tracks, envelopes, or effects.

Applying opacity to video groups

You can adjust the opacity of a video group in two ways—either by adjusting the group's **Opacity** slider in the group's Properties pane, or by adjusting a group's opacity on its opacity envelope. For the latter method, click the 🔽 **Attributes** button in the group header to reveal the **Attributes** menu—select Opacity to reveal an editable inline opacity envelope. This will allow you to fade the result of an affected section of video organized within a group, for instance, or to make a series of still image overlays appear translucent—without having to edit each clip or track in an identical way.

See Using envelopes on p. 90 for more information about revealing and editing envelopes in general.

Transforms—perspective, scaling, and motion

You can apply transforms, such as perspective effects, resizing, or animated motion, to video groups. Such an effect would allow for the composite result of a group to be used as an inset video, for instance. To learn how to edit a transform envelope, see Adjusting keyframes on p. 95.

Master groups

Show Master Groups (**View** menu) lets you affect all the video groups and video tracks separately but in one fell swoop. For example, you could apply a video effect to all videos in your project by applying it to the master group.

The Master Group appears in your timeline header and contains all your tracks.

Video effect groups

Video effect groups are not used frequently but are essential if you wish to blend affected and unaffected video. The affected video would have cumulative effects applied, which could be blended in and out of the mix by adjusting the keyframes of the Video Effect Group's envelope. See p. 133.

Audio effect groups

The audio equivalent of video effect groups. See p. 145.

Trimming clips on the timeline

You can perform multi-trimming via the Timeline toolbar's **Trim** button (see p. 32) or directly on the timeline.

To trim a clip on the timeline directly:

1. Hover your cursor over the start (or end) of your clip so that the cursor changes (to ⊣⊢ or ⊣⊢).

2. Click and drag to the right (or left) to trim away the start (or end) of your clip.

To trim accurately, position your time indicator at the exact position you want to trim to, then drag the start (or end) of your clip to the time indicator.

Splitting clips on the timeline

The **Trim** option in the Media pane allows you to split a clip into separate scenes before adding to the timeline. However, you can still split any video clip once on the timeline at the currently set time indicator's position.

Splitting a clip into two lets you insert another "filler" clip in between each split clip. You can perform multiple splits to create distinct sections of your clips for deletion.

To split a clip:

1. Select the clip you would like to split.

2. Position the time indicator on the ruler at the point in the clip where you'd like to make the split.

3. Click ✂ **Split** on the Timeline toolbar.

> 🔍 If you have no clip selected, all clips across tracks are split at the time indicator.

Cropping

You can perform simple crops on any clip by using the ▭ **Fit** button in either Storyboard or Timeline mode (See Resizing clips on p. 50). This affects the clip for its entire duration. However, the power of the Timeline mode lets you change a clip's cropping over time (just as for transforming a clip).

The method for cropping and transforming over time is similar in the way it is applied, i.e. like a transform, cropping uses a dedicated envelope, which is accessible for any clip from the clip's Attributes menu. This **crop envelope** is displayed, controlled and modified as for any other envelope. It can host one or more keyframes along the envelopes length (called the strip) to dictate the crop selection area, i.e. each keyframe sets the crop area size at that time.

For a quick recap on envelopes and keyframes, see Using envelopes and Adjusting keyframes on p. 90 and p. 95.

MoviePlus opens up some interesting possibilities when cropping over time as you can pan in any direction, zoom, pan/zoom together and create panoramas. To make life easier, you can perform the above operations by adopting a pre-built crop envelope preset.

To use a crop envelope preset:

1. Select a clip and choose **Apply Envelope...** from the **Insert** menu.

2. From the dialog, pick the Crop folder, a crop preset from any child folder, then click on a preset under that folder.

3. Click **OK**.

You'll notice the crop envelope appear under your clip.

The envelope typically shows two keyframes, each storing the crop area's size at that time. The properties of the selected keyframe (●) show the sized crop area.

You can modify the envelope by adjusting the crop area on each keyframe in the envelope, and optionally saving the preset to a new name.

Alternatively, you can set the crop area manually by entering Top, Bottom, Left or Right percentage values (click the **Manual** drop-down option).

To save your modified envelope:

*   Click 🖫 **Add to Gallery** in the envelope's Properties pane. You'll be asked for an envelope name. The envelope is saved to the root Crop folder of the Envelope dialog (or Galleries pane).

Cropping with masks

As a very powerful way of cropping irregular shaped objects (as opposed to cropping to square or rectangle areas), cropping video with masks involves using a simple image overlay to describe which areas of your video should remain visible and which areas should become transparent.

Masks are usually simple images made with a transparent region and a white region; when applied correctly in the MoviePlus timeline, these images affect underlying video, with white in the mask translating to visible regions of your video and transparency in your mask translating to transparent (cut/cropped) regions of the video. You can use this functionality to hide (or crop away) portions of your video that you do not want included. Masks allow for irregular cropping, cropping with soft edges, animated cropping; the possibilities are infinite, as are the number of mask images or videos you can create.

For more information see Masks on p. 114.

Using envelopes

Envelopes in this context are not an item of stationery, they are a method of applying change to a clip, track or group's properties over time. Imagine an envelope as a hidden "track" that runs along with each clip, track, and group in your project and at specific times you determine how it changes its properties. Between the specific times you specify envelope settings, MoviePlus can calculate smooth changes to the properties.

There are different types of envelopes that all work in very similar ways for controlling cropping, opacity, and transforms for video clips, and volume and stereo pan for audio clips. Once you learn how to display and modify one type of envelope, you can apply the same principle to all other envelope types. However there is a distinction between some envelope types.

- **Opacity**, **Volume** and **Pan**: These simple envelopes can adjust the properties of an object over its duration on the timeline. They appear as thick strips because the envelope only affects one attribute (e.g., volume level). This lets you position buttons (called keyframes) in the vertical axis to create fade-ins or fade-outs of opacity, volume and pan. For example, a volume envelope could be used on an audio track to fade-in the sound at the start of your video.

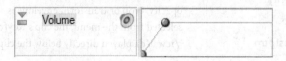

- **Crop** and **Transform**: These more complex envelopes can also adjust the properties of an object over the timeline, but as they possess multiple properties which are often inter-related, they can't be easily represented on the timeline. Therefore, they appear as a thin strip stretching the duration of the clip, track or group, leaving the envelope's Properties pane to take on the configuration role.

Envelopes can be edited, copied, pasted and muted (to temporarily switch off its effect). Editing of the envelope is possible on the whole envelope or on individual keyframes within the envelope itself.

Displaying envelopes

Envelopes can be displayed as strips that show under the selected clip, track or group. Choose from the options below:

For clips

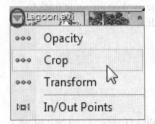

Click on the ⏷ button on top of your clip to reveal an **Attributes** menu. When an opacity, crop or transform envelope is selected from the menu, the clip's **Keyframe View** is displayed directly below the clip.

All envelopes are shown in separate strips with your chosen envelope already selected. To change to a different envelope either click another envelope's name in the video header or click anywhere in the envelope strip on the timeline.

The ⏷ button, being grey/white, will change colour to red/white when selected. If your envelope has been modified it will adopt a red/yellow colour.

For video tracks and groups

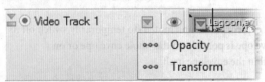

Click on the ⏷ button in the header section of a selected track or group to reveal an **Attributes** menu. Like clips, selected envelopes and keyframes show under track or group.

Adjustments to envelopes will affect all clips on the track, or all tracks in the group. For example, adjustments to a video group's opacity envelope will result in opacity changes to the composite result of the group's contents. For example, if a video group contains four tracks each with a transform envelope that makes each track fill just one quarter of the visible area, all four videos would simultaneously have their opacity adjusted when you modify their group's opacity envelope. Groups are also used when cropping or masking video, so you may want to adjust the group's opacity—rather than individual tracks or clips.

Preset envelopes

MoviePlus provides a great selection of preset crop, opacity, and transform (video/image) and volume and pan envelopes (audio) to apply to your clips, tracks or groups. Use the presets to get you started or to simply save you time.

To apply an envelope preset:

1. Select the clip, track or group.

2. From the Attributes menu, select Opacity, Crop (clip only), or Transform to show its envelope.

3. From the Properties pane, select **Gallery....**

4. From the dialog, navigate the tree menu structure and choose a preset envelope. Your envelope shows automatically under the object.

5. Click **OK**.

Editing envelopes

All envelopes are powerful because of the potential to manipulate existing or added keyframes along the envelope's length. This keyframe control is at the heart of not only envelope management, but also the management of effects and transitions, and is described in detail in Adjusting keyframes (see p. 95).

All envelopes have one default keyframe positioned at the start of the object, which defines how the envelope will operate either until the next keyframe on the timeline or for the duration of the clip, track or group.

Resetting envelopes

An envelope cannot be deleted but instead its resident keyframes can be deleted, effectively resetting the envelope back to its default state. Simply select the envelope and press the **Delete** key.

Copying and scaling envelopes

An envelope can be copied by right-clicking on its header and choosing **Copy**. When an envelope is copied to the clipboard, it can be pasted to another selected object to replace the existing envelope of that object, e.g. an opacity envelope from one clip will overwrite the opacity envelope of another video clip by copy and paste.

If an envelope is copied and pasted from one clip to another clip further down the timeline, associated keyframes can be optionally scaled so they are in proportion with the new clip. This is also useful if you are changing the total length of the track as the key frames are scaled to that new length. To do this, change each keyframe's **Keyframe Mode** to Proportional in the envelope's Properties pane. Another advantage of scaling is that you can save your own custom envelope to a new preset, safe in the knowledge that the keyframes are never stored with absolute times, and instead can be scaled easily to any object on the timeline in the future!

Saving envelopes

To save your envelope to a new name (in the Properties pane) along with your existing presets, use the **Add to Gallery** button in the envelope's Properties pane. After providing a name, your new envelope is saved in the envelope type's root folder.

Adjusting keyframes (timeline only)

The Keyframe View

When you add an envelope, effect or transition to a clip, track, or group, the **Keyframe View** is displayed directly underneath the object as a white area, e.g. for a clip.

When you want to edit an existing envelope, effect or transition, click on the grey/white button on your object to reveal a drop-down **Attributes** menu. On selecting a menu item, the object's currently applied envelopes, effects and/or transitions are shown in one or more strips directly under the object (the button changes to red/white). Each strip allows you to induce change over time, whether it's for an envelope, effect or transition. The points in time that you specify such change are represented on these strips by **keyframes** (● or ● when selected).

The Attributes button will change to red/yellow (🔽) if an envelope, effect or transition has been edited and then to grey/yellow when a modified object has all its strips hidden.

Once the Keyframe View is enabled, you will be able to edit envelopes and their keyframes, causing change over time.

What are keyframes?

A keyframe is the small grey circle that appears on the envelope, effect or transition strips. For tracks and groups there is a default keyframe at the start of the timeline. For selected clips, the default keyframe is set at the start of the clip, so when you move your clip its envelope also moves in synchronization.

Keyframes store information about the property you are editing. If we use opacity as an example, as it's such a simple property, MoviePlus draws a line of a set height along the length of its envelope to describe whether the current opacity value is high, low, or any stage in between (as shown).

The initial single keyframe defines the opacity level by its vertical position in the envelope (see how the Properties pane's Opacity value changes as you drag the keyframe up and down).

You can modify keyframe properties when a keyframe is selected—click a grey (deselected) keyframe and it will turn red (selected).

Modifying the default keyframe

To modify the default keyframe you can either move it up and down within the strip (for some simple envelopes) or just click the keyframe to select it (it will turn red) then adjust its properties in the Properties pane (for complex envelopes, effects, or transitions). You can also move the keyframe further along the timeline to the right.

 An important point about the first and last keyframes when moved is that their properties will extend to the beginning and end of the clip, track, or group.

Adding and modifying keyframes

To cause change over time (by changing an object's properties), it is essential to add and subsequently edit keyframes along the attribute's strip (for crops, transforms, effects, and transitions). For effects and transitions you'll need to apply them in advance.

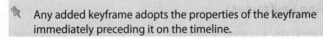 Any added keyframe adopts the properties of the keyframe immediately preceding it on the timeline.

To add a keyframe:

1. (Optional) Position your time indicator for accurate keyframe placement.

2. Select the attribute from the Attributes menu (click ▼).

3. In the strip's header, select the attribute to add a keyframe to.

4. Hover the cursor along the object's strip until it changes to the Add cursor (+), then click to add the keyframe. If you've positioned your time indicator, hover over the point where the indicator intersects with the strip—you'll add a keyframe that snaps to an exact time.

You can also use ⁺⊙ **Add Keyframe** on the Properties pane; this adds a keyframe at the current time indicator's position.

Whichever way keyframes are added, they can be arranged along a strip at chosen intervals (a keyframe is red when selected).

For some simpler envelopes such as opacity, pan and volume, you can add and edit keyframes as above but you can also drag the keyframe up or down to adjust the keyframe's properties directly. These envelope strips are designed to have more depth for this reason—great for fade-in and fade-outs on opacity and volume envelopes.

In this example, a volume envelope on an Audio track fades in at the start of a movie. MoviePlus draws the rate of volume change as a line between the keyframes.

Any keyframe can be modified via the Properties pane—simply select the keyframe (making it red) and display the Properties pane for editing.

Selecting keyframes

At some point you may want to select more than one keyframe at the same time—typically to cut, copy, or move keyframes. You can also change Interpolation or Keyframe Mode by right-clicking on multiple keyframes and accessing a flyout menu. MoviePlus lets you select multiple keyframes as for any other object on the timeline.

- Use **Ctrl**-click to select each keyframe in turn.
  OR

- Drag a marquee around a region containing your keyframes.

Moving keyframes

You can move one or more selected keyframes left and right along the strip which has the effect of moving them earlier or later along the timeline. For more precision, you can also set a selected **Keyframe time** position in the Properties pane.

Navigating keyframes

- Use the **Ctrl+<** and **Ctrl+>** keyboard shortcuts to **Select Previous Keyframe** and **Select Next Keyframe** on a strip (also available on the **Transport** menu).
  OR

- Use the button in the Properties pane.

Copying keyframes

Any selected keyframe can be copied to the clipboard. Simply select a single keyframe (or multiple keyframes with the **Ctrl** key), right-click and select **Copy**.

When keyframes are on the clipboard, they can be pasted into any attribute strip of the same type they came from. They will be pasted at the time indicator location.

If an envelope, effect or transition is copied and pasted from one clip to another clip further down the timeline, associated keyframes can be optionally scaled so they are in proportion with the new clip. This is also useful if you are changing the total length of the track as the keyframes are scaled to that new length. To do this, change each keyframe's **Keyframe Mode** to Proportional in the envelope's, effect's or transition's Properties pane. Another advantage of scaling is that you can save your own custom envelope, effect or transition to a new preset, safe in the knowledge that the keyframes are never stored with absolute times, and instead can be scaled easily to any object on the timeline in the future!

Altering rate of change between keyframes

By default, where you have two keyframes with different values, MoviePlus will gradually step from one range of settings to the next in a smooth manner—this is known as Linear interpolation. MoviePlus is interpolating (calculating) values between the keyframes and the change is linear, i.e. half way between the values you will have encountered half the required amount of change.

However, it's handy to be able to alter the rate of change, as in video production it's usually a good idea to aim for smoothness—sudden starts or ends to movement (as with other effects) is not always desirable and can sometimes detract from the video content.

To alter the rate of change between keyframes:

1. Right-click a keyframe, to view the **Interpolation** flyout. This offers handy previews of the rates of change as curved or straight lines, like a graph or chart.
   OR

   Select a keyframe, and in the keyframe's Properties pane, click the **More** option to reveal keyframe properties.

2. Choose an interpolation method via the **Interpolation** option.

Using the volume envelope example below, a right-click on the first keyframe will allow you to adjust the rate of volume change towards the second keyframe—a curve appears between keyframes.

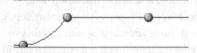

The first keyframe is subject to a Quadratic Slow curve to start and end the fade-in slowly.

On occasion, you may wish to apply a Hold interpolation on a keyframe where, instead of change over time, the keyframe's properties remain constant for its duration. These are particularly useful on an audio clip's volume envelope where you may want to switch the volume on and off at specific points along the timeline (instead of fading).

Positioning keyframes

When you modify an object or you intend to copy and paste an attribute's strip to another object's attribute strip (of different length) you can choose various mode options to decide how MoviePlus will reposition a keyframe once it is copied.

- For an envelope, effect, or transition, the **Keyframe Mode** setting offers various positioning options for keyframes; this affects only the **currently selected** keyframe(s).

The Keyframe Mode settings, found by right-clicking the Keyframe or from the **More** section of the attribute's Properties pane, can be one of the following:

- **Absolute**: Selected Keyframe does not move (default). Great for corresponding your keyframes to an event on the timeline.

- **Proportional**: Selected Keyframe moves in proportion to the new object's length (i.e., duration). Useful for creating presets (e.g., envelopes) whose keyframes will scale to any target object.

- **Relative to Start**: Keyframe will move relative to the start of the strip if the object's length is changed. Use for fade-ins.

- **Relative to End**: Keyframe will move relative to the end of the strip if the object's length is changed. Use for fade-outs.

- **Proportional (excl. transitions)**: As for Proportional, but applies only to the clip's inner range excluding transitions.

- **Relative to Start (excl. transitions)**: As for Relative to Start, but applies only to the clip's inner range excluding transitions.

- **Relative to End (excl. transitions)**: As for Relative to End, but applies only to the clip's inner range excluding transitions.

If you want to apply the same Keyframe Mode to multiple keyframes, you can select your keyframes (see Selecting keyframes), right-click, and pick a new setting from the flyout menu.

> When keyframes have a **Keyframe mode** of "Absolute" they are affected by Rippling (if turned on). Other modes will be unaffected by rippling.

Applying transitions (timeline)

Any time one piece of video ends and another begins, a transition takes place. In its simplest form, the transition is simply a cut: in less than the blink of an eye, the last frame of a clip is replaced by the first frame of a second clip.

In MoviePlus, the term "transition" applies to a more gradual way of switching from one clip to another. If you add multiple media files from the Media pane or overlap two clips slightly on the same or separate tracks, you get a time-based change between them, shown as a blue region. An In transition called "Cross-Fade" is added by default to the second clip.

For audio, an equivalent transition is added to fade the audio from the first to the second audio clip.

> The default Cross-Fade and Fade transition types have no associated properties. However, all other transition types have associated properties, which can be modified at any time.

Changing transition type

MoviePlus offers an impressive selection of transition types that you can swap your default transition for. Types range from 3D blinds, bands, wipes, fades, slides, spirals, and more.

To change transition type:

1. Select one or more transitions on the timeline.

    *   For specific transitions, **Ctrl**-click on each clip's transition region one-by-one. This can be carried out across multiple tracks if needed.

    *   For all transitions on a single track, select any single transition on the track, then press **Ctrl+A**.

    *   For all transitions across multiple tracks, select a transition on each of the tracks (with **Ctrl**-click), then press **Ctrl+A**.

2. Click **Transition Gallery** on the context toolbar.

3. From the dialog, choose a category from the upper window. In the lower window, review the presets available (their names indicate their intended function). Select a preset, e.g. 3D Page Roll.

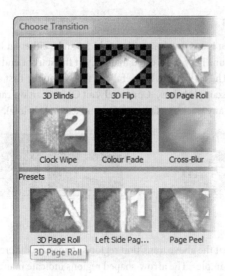

4. Click **OK**.

The Transition name(s) changes, e.g. from "Cross-Fade" to "3D Page Roll":

The end of the first clip is indicated by the vertical dashed red line.

  For a quick way to replace transitions, display the Galleries pane, select the **Transitions** tab, then drag and drop a transition thumbnail onto your transition.

Manual transitions

Another type of transition is a manual transition, which can be either an In transition or Out transition. They are created manually at the start or end of a single clip, respectively. The former can be useful as a fade-in on the first clip at the start of a track (first example below). Conversely, an Out transition can be applied to the last clip in any track as a fade-out (second example below).

In Transition   *Out Transition*

You may have noticed that the above transition region's shapes are different compared to previous examples. The arrow-shaped regions indicate manual transitions—the arrow is actually a handle to drag left or right to adjust the transition's duration.

To change a manual transition's duration:

Drag the left or right-hand end (as shown below) of the transition region to stretch or shrink it, or specify an absolute value in the transition's Properties pane.

Remember that each transition takes time to happen—so make sure the video in the overlap region is not part of the main action. If you expect to use transitions, it's a good idea to allow a couple of seconds of non-essential material at the start and end of clips when you initially capture them.

 The duration of Automatic transitions is altered automatically by moving either clip on the timeline.

You can also modify the transition duration of one or more automatic or manual transitions using the Properties pane's **Duration** option.

Modifying transitions

Transitions added to your project will have their own set of properties associated with them. These are highly customizable via the **Properties** pane, just like any other object in MoviePlus. Try selecting a transition region and check its properties in the Properties Pane.

The ability to customize transitions by changing these property settings means that the presets supplied are merely a starting point for you to further create and save your own transitions to your own requirements.

To modify a transition:

1. Select the transition region.

2. From the transition's Properties pane, alter the transition' properties at the bottom of the pane.

To save a modified transition to a new name:

- Click the **Add to Gallery** button at the top of the Properties pane. Once named, the transition appears as a new preset in the appropriate folder in the Choose Transition dialog (or Transitions tab in the Galleries pane).

Overlaps

The overlap is the region in between overlapping clips where the transition will be visible.

The overlap region is the area between the start of the second clip and a red vertical dashed line indicating the end of the first clip.

Overlap control is especially useful when creating photo slideshows in MoviePlus. Even though your added clips will have a set overlap shown between them, you can modify an individual or selected clip's overlap easily.

To change the clip overlap:

1. Select the clips on your track(s).

2. From the Timeline context toolbar, enter an **Overlap** value.

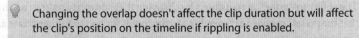

Changing the overlap doesn't affect the clip duration but will affect the clip's position on the timeline if rippling is enabled.

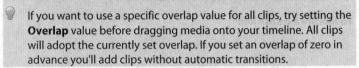

If you want to use a specific overlap value for all clips, try setting the **Overlap** value before dragging media onto your timeline. All clips will adopt the currently set overlap. If you set an overlap of zero in advance you'll add clips without automatic transitions.

Adjusting transition properties

A transition, when applied, possesses a single keyframe which dictates the transition duration, interpolation, and settings particular to the type of transition, e.g. blur, transition direction, etc. This applies a uniform setting throughout the transition's duration.

A single keyframe is shown in a Transition strip, shown directly below the clip when double-clicking the transition region (double-click again to hide the strip). In and Out transitions are shown in separate strips with your chosen transition already selected. For example, for an automatic In transition "3D Page Roll" and manual Out transition "Iris Wipe" applied to a single clip:

By clicking on the keyframe (the button on each strip) on either transition, the properties of the transition can be modified for the duration of the transition (you alter each keyframe's properties in the Properties pane). The duration of automatic transitions cannot be modified.

If one keyframe is modified the change is applied over the transition's duration. However, more exciting transitions can be made by changing your transition over time.

Applying transitions over time

It is possible to specify how a transition alters throughout its duration by setting keyframes at different points on its strip, but only within the transition's duration (and not over a whole clip or track). The strip allows keyframes to be place along its length, which can be modified in turn to define how a transition's properties are to be applied at that point in the transition. A 3D Page Roll transition could have a second keyframe (with different properties) added at the end of the transition, to allow the transition to change over time.

During video preview, as the time indicator passes along the timeline the video's transition will change over time by using the differing properties of the last visited keyframe and the next keyframe on the timeline. The transition can be interpolated linearly or can adopt different types of quadratic or cubic algorithms to effect different rates of change.

Keyframe control is described in Adjusting keyframes (see p. 95).

Snapping

If **Snapping** is enabled (**Arrange** menu), the transition will conveniently fit into the overlap region. If snapping is disabled, or you drag the transition to an overlapping area between tracks, it will adopt a default overlap time as set in **Tools>Options>Editing**. Any applied transition should always match the overlap region, i.e. where two clips are co-existing on the timeline.

When snapping is enabled, your clips will be "sticky" when you drag clips near the default overlap period (MoviePlus offers a 1-second sticky overlap point by default). This makes it easy to keep a standard transition duration throughout your project without manually editing each transition duration in the Properties pane (or very carefully dragging your clips) for each overlap; MoviePlus uses standard values which you can alter in the **Tools>Options>Editing** dialog. The overlap value is also used as a default transition duration when you add multiple image clips to the timeline simultaneously—great for making quick slide shows!

Using markers

Markers have several uses in MoviePlus but are always added along the top of your timeline at the current time indicator. Three types of marker are available:

Marker 1	**Basic marker** (green) Used as simple reference points, to indicate important events occurring at key times in your movie, e.g. sound or action, or to mark the start and end of clips on more complex multi-track projects (for positioning and arranging).
Chapter 1	**Chapter point** (blue) For use exclusively when creating menus for discs, they exist in two forms standard or Top Level; The former define the beginning of chapters on any menu; the latter, the chapter points on the Top Level menu only (see Menu Designer: Editing chapter properties on p. 194).
Selection Start Selection End	**Selection markers** (blue) Define a time range for selective pre-rendering or to export only part of your MoviePlus project (to file, PSP, or iTunes).

> Markers of any type are coloured orange on selection.

Using markers

Markers of any type can be added at any point on your timeline—they can be labelled, repositioned by dragging, as well as navigated.

To insert a marker:

1. Click on the timeline ruler to set the time indicator's position.

2. From the context toolbar's [icon] **Marker** drop-down list choose:

    - **Insert Marker**.
      OR

    - **Insert Chapter Point**.
      OR

    - **Set Selection Start** (or **End**).

By default, markers will be named according to type, i.e. Marker 1, Marker 2, Chapter 1, Chapter 2, Selection Start, etc.

To rename your marker:

    - Go to the selected marker's Properties pane and edit the **Marker** field.

To select a marker:

    - Click the marker box (whether a basic marker, chapter point, or selection marker) on the timeline ruler (use **Ctrl**-click to select multiple markers; or **Ctrl+A** to select all markers).

To delete a marker:

    - Click on the marker and press **Delete**.

Navigating markers

If you're working on a long timeline you may need to navigate your markers so you can check that each marker is of the correct type and position. The navigation method is the same for any marker type (basic, chapter point, or selection marker).

To navigate markers one by one:

- With any marker selected, use **Ctrl+Shift**+left or **Ctrl+Shift**+right arrow keys

To navigate markers via dialog:

- From the context toolbar's [icon] **Marker** drop-down list, select **Go to Marker...** to select from markers (of any type) listed in a dialog.

Using chapter points

Chapter points are a type of marker used to define where chapters play from in your generated disc—much the same as the initial menu shown in any movie DVD from your local movie store. When you decide to create your disc, these named chapters will be shown as menu thumbnails that can be clicked to play the movie from that point.

In the Menu Designer, chapter points inserted in your timeline will be detected and the associated chapters will be thumbnailed automatically (see Menu Designer on p. 190).

MoviePlus supports multi-level menus, where you can store your main chapters on the top-level menu (first page) while subsidiary chapters can be made to appear on a secondary menu (second page). For the former, select **Top Level** in the Properties pane for any chapter point you want on the top level. Any other chapter points (with Top Level unselected) appear on the secondary menu. Optionally, add alternative title text that will display next to your menu's thumbnail label. Otherwise, the Marker name is used as the menu label.

> In Storyboard mode, chapter points can be inserted at the start of any clip by clicking the thumbnail's **Chapter Point** button.

As an example of chapter points on the timeline, a holiday movie could have named chapter points which represent key points on the movie, e.g. Castle, Dolphins, Flamingo, etc.

> If you want to convert a basic marker to a chapter point, simply select **chapter point** in the selected marker's Properties pane, and set the additional chapter point options as required.

Using selection markers

Selection markers differ slightly from basic markers and chapter points. Instead, they work in pairs to set a time range on your timeline within which MoviePlus can perform operations limited to that set range. Operations include:

- Pre-rendering part of the timeline that contains complex MoviePlus-applied effects and transitions, for improved preview playback.

- Exporting a part of your movie by setting an export range. Used for exporting to file, PSP, or iTunes (for video-capable Apple devices).

To limit to a specific time range:

1. Click on the timeline ruler to set the time indicator's position.

2. From the context toolbar's **Marker** drop-down menu, choose **Set Selection Start** (or right-click on the time indicator) to set the start of your time range. From the same menu, select **Set Selection End** to set the end of your range.

3. (Optional) Drag your **Selection Start** and **Selection End** markers along the timeline to fine-tune your time range.

Once set, any pre-rendering or exporting will be limited to the chosen time range. Pre-rendering is carried out with the **Pre-render Selected Range** option (**Preview** menu).

Slowing down and speeding up

Video clips can be slowed down (slow motion) or speeded up by decreasing or increasing the **Play speed** on the clip's Properties pane. You'll see the duration change on the chosen clip as you adjust this value—when a video plays slower or faster, it has a longer or shorter duration, respectively. Image or text clips cannot have their **Play speed** adjusted.

On the timeline, you can still adjust the **Play speed** as described above but to increase or decrease the play speed, hold the **Ctrl** key down and drag an edge of your video clip inwards or outwards, respectively.

Transparency & opacity (timeline only)

Transparency and opacity are intrinsically linked, like different sides of the same coin. Opacity means a state of being opaque—you cannot see through a video or other clip to those underneath if it is totally opaque. By contrast of course, you can see through video that is partially or wholly transparent, or has regions that are partially or wholly transparent, with no opacity.

Text clip over video clip
(90% opacity)

Text clip over video clip
(60% opacity)

MoviePlus generally refers to opacity rather than transparency, but you should keep both concepts in mind during your editing to help understand various features such as Chroma Key (matting/blue screening) and masks.

Let's firstly take a look at different ways in which opacity can be used on whole clips, tracks, groups and effects in MoviePlus. A general level of opacity can be applied to:

- a clip, to allow you to "fade" video or images in and out of vision over other video clips.

- a whole video track, to make a collection of clips more or less visible.

- a video group, so that the composite result of a collection of grouped tracks can be made less or more visible as part of the overall composition.

- a video effect group (i.e., allowing **mix back** to blend original with affected video).

For all of the above, an opacity envelope is used to set a constant level of opacity or to alter opacity over time for that object. See Using envelopes and Adjusting keyframes on p. 90 and 95 for more information.

A specific region of transparency or opacity can be created for:

- Removing a solid-coloured background (also called blue- or green-screening). This is achieved using a video effect called Chroma Key.

- Creating a cut-out region, using a mask.

- Creating a limited region for an effect to be applied over, e.g. only applying a mosaic effect to a subject's face rather than the whole video, also using a mask.

- Cropping using a mask.

For a preface to the concepts involved in removing a specific region of video, see Removing backgrounds on p. 114.

Removing Backgrounds

There are a number of reasons you might want to "remove" a region of your video:

- To isolate a foreground subject in order to place them against a different background, e.g. blue-screening such as used for movie special effects and daily favourites like weather presenting.

- To cut out a hole in a video, e.g. a billboard advertising area or sports stadium big screen, in order to place a video of your own in the cut out region.

- To limit the extent of an effect e.g. to just mosaic someone's face to respect their privacy but leave the remainder of the video unaffected.

- To crop your movie, e.g. leave just a rectangular or other-shaped portion of your video and discard the remainder, perhaps leaving room for other cropped videos on screen to sit alongside to form a montage, popularized by comic book hero movies.

The cutting out of regular shapes and cropping of video is something you can achieve using masks. The removal of a solid-coloured background can be achieved using a Chroma Key effect, also called blue-screening/green-screening, matting, colour keying and colour separation overlays.

Masking

Masks are a way of using an image to "cut out" a rectangular or other-shaped portion from a video, leaving transparency around the subject, effectively removing a background to give focus to a foreground element. You can also use masks to crop video for multiple picture-in-picture effects. Masks can also remove a foreground element to reveal another video or image clip through the cut-out region.

Masks as used in MoviePlus are best created as transparent images with a white region to indicate the shape of underlying video to keep; the white region is like the inside shape of a cookie cutter, the transparent region is discarded like the outlying pastry around your cutter. You can also use images that contain a mixture of different colours and transparent regions for advanced masking.

In addition, QuickShapes let you apply shaped masks directly onto the timeline with no fuss. See Using CG clips on p. 57.

 You can create your own masks with Serif PhotoPlus.

You can see the result of combining a "heart" mask with a video clip, each stored on separate video tracks.

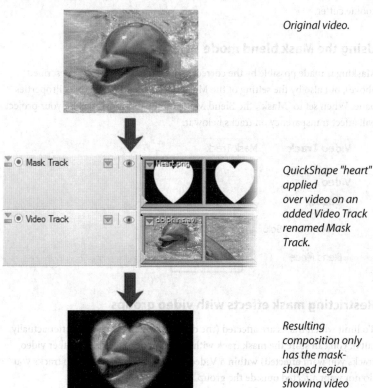

Original video.

QuickShape "heart" applied over video on an added Video Track renamed Mask Track.

Resulting composition only has the mask-shaped region showing video content.

Try out some different QuickShapes by dragging them from the Media pane's Library tab (Samples folder).

Masks should be added to separately created tracks.

Video tracks

Before you go ahead and add a mask to your timeline, it's useful to know in advance how masks and the organization of your video tracks work together. Masks need to occupy a track of their own to have an effect on underlying video compositions... the mask's white regions determine which regions of underlying video clips you see—the mask sits on top of other video clips to act as a virtual cookie cutter.

Using the Mask blend mode

Masking is made possible by the correct arrangement of tracks (as described above), but also by the setting of the Mask track's **Blend Mode** in its Properties pane. When set to "**Mask**", the Blend Mode on the top-most track in your project will affect transparency on tracks below it.

Restricting mask effects with video groups

To limit which tracks are affected (the depth to which the cookie cutter actually cuts), you can store the mask track with blend mode applied (and other video tracks you want affected) within a Video Group, leaving other video tracks you do not want affected outside the group.

Looking at the track names in the example below, "Holiday Track 2" is not subject to the heart-shaped clipping that the Mask Track is performing because it is outside the video group—the mask's effect is limited to tracks within its video group, i.e. the Main Holiday Track only.

The Main Holiday Track footage is masked as it is in the same group as Mask Track; Holiday Track 2 is kept outside Video Group 1.

The mask only cuts out content from the image of the dolphin. The underlying video, outside of the video group, is unaffected by the masking operation!

Creating your own masks

To create a mask it is recommended you use a bitmap (photo) editing program that fully supports transparency, such as Serif PhotoPlus. Some other programs that can easily create shapes with or without soft edges (and can export images with transparency, such as 32-bit PNG) are also useful for creating masks—Serif DrawPlus is an example.

You should aim to use white to create the region you wish to maintain in your video, and transparency for the areas you wish to cut away. Partial transparency is supported, so you can create regions of translucency as well as using a mask to create solid regions of opacity and transparency in your video.

> Remember to create your masks at a suitable size for your project, taking pixel aspect ratio into account if your project's pixel aspect ratio is not set to 1. As a quick guide, you should multiply the project's pixel aspect ratio x frame width = width you need to create your mask.

To add your own masks to your project, browse to their saved location using the Media pane, and drag your mask image onto a track of its own, positioned above the video you would like to mask.

Once in your project, you can also stretch your mask to fit using **Stretch** from the **Fit** drop-down menu on the Timeline context toolbar. Alternatively, you can always adjust size and position using a transform envelope (see p. 90).

Blue/green screening (Chroma Key)

This process, referred to as Chroma Key in MoviePlus, enjoys a few other names including colour keying, matting, and colour separation overlay. It is a method of removing a colour (or a colour range) from one video or image to reveal another video or image behind it. The "removed" colour becomes transparent.

This process is commonly used for weather broadcasts and of course in many movie blockbusters. To start with, the foreground subject—a weather presenter for instance—is filmed against a solid-coloured and evenly-illuminated backdrop. Using MoviePlus (or expensive studio wizardry in the case of live TV weather slots), the solid coloured region of this video can be made transparent using a Chroma Key effect, revealing an underlying video. In the case of some weather presenting, the video "behind" the presenter can show a weather map with animated symbols or weather systems. In movies, the process saves actors being put in dangerous positions, such as visually-stunning explosions, or in places that cannot be reached for practical or budgetary reasons, such as across the other side of the globe or in space.

It's not only a background that can be removed; you can, for instance, hold up a solid-coloured card while being filmed and later remove that solid colour from the video to create a card-shaped cut-out. The alternate "background" video would then display through this "hole".

Blue screening in action

Simple blue-screen filming of a "skiing" family against a solid-coloured background (e.g., a blue studio backdrop).

Background video, placed on the track below the blue-screen footage on the timeline.

The upper video clip on the timeline, the blue-screen footage, has had a Chroma Key effect applied to it. Properties sliders were adjusted to remove all the blue.

Applying the Chroma Key effect

Effects in MoviePlus can be applied to individual video clips, whole tracks, or video groups. While Chroma Key can also be applied to all three hierarchies, it is most commonly used with individual video clips, as it is not usual for there to be multiple clips with the same background colour to be made transparent.

The effect is applied like any other video effect, from the *fx* **Effects** button on the Timeline context toolbar (see Applying video effects on p. 133).

The Chroma Key effect will automatically remove whichever colour is associated with the Chroma Key effect applied to your video. For example, if you use the "Blue screen" preset then the preset's colour (RGB 0,0,255) is removed if present in your video clip. You'll more than likely need to accurately make your effect colour to be the same as your blue screening backdrop colour:

To change the Chroma Key colour:

1. Display the effect's Properties pane.

2. Either:

   - Use the colour picker to select a new colour value from the upper clip that you want to remove (hold down the mouse button, and drag the picker over the colour you require, and release). This would normally be the backdrop colour.
     OR

   - Define a new colour by clicking the **Colour** spectrum and, from the **Adjust Colour** dialog, select an RGB, HSL or HTML code.

Changing thresholds and blurring

MoviePlus lets you fine-tune the Chroma Key effect to help the colour-detection processes determine which bits of your video to make transparent. It is very useful to be able to set a **Low** and **High** threshold for colour detection—this transparency is set according to brightness levels. **Blur** lets you blur the shape of the transparent region generated by the Chroma Key effect.

Changing the Chroma Key effect over time

You can adjust the Chroma Key settings so that they change over time, perhaps to account for a change in lighting conditions that affects the colour you're trying to remove. Your Chroma Key effect can start by removing pale blue and slowly change to removing a stronger blue, for instance.

For more information, see Adjusting keyframes on p. 95.

Video overlays (timeline only)

You can "layer" all sorts of different kinds of clips on top of existing video or image clips—this flexibility opens up a world of possibilities in your video production.

Overlays, in basic terms, are two or more clips being displayed at once, one on top of the other—these clips are layered on multiple video tracks. For the bottom clip to still be visible despite having another clip on top of it, the top clips need to:

- be smaller than the bottom clip.

- have transparent regions.

- have reduced opacity.

Top clip made smaller

When you add an opaque clip to the upper track, it is likely to occlude clips on lower tracks completely, so all you can see is the content of the top-most track. To see "around it" to underlying clips you can resize your top clip by using a Transform envelope on the upper clip or track. You can also reshape your clip, deform with perspective and even animate the resizing or reshaping process. See Introducing Transforms to learn more.

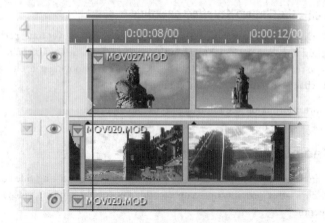

Timeline

Video preview—before transform

Video preview—after transform

Top clip has transparent regions

Overlaid video

In the example above, the top clip was completely opaque and therefore obscured all video underneath it. However, when you add a video with transparent regions to the upper track, the content of underlying tracks will be seen through the upper clip's transparent regions. We've added a sample from the **Library** tab on the **Media** pane to make the above example more compelling.

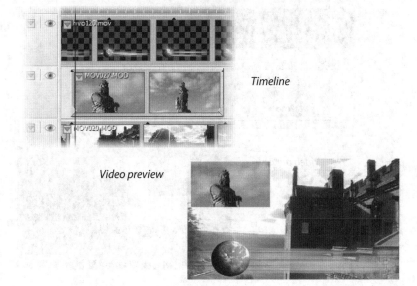

Timeline

Video preview

Overlaid STV video

You can make your own overlay animations and effects using Serif DrawPlus, if you export your keyframe animations as **Serif Transparent Video** (STV). Remember to choose the STV format to export with a transparent background!

When you add an STV video file to a track above existing video or images, MoviePlus will smoothly overlay the STV on top, revealing underlying clips through the video's transparent region(s).

Overlaid images

If the image on the top track has built-in transparency you will automatically be able to see through the transparent region to any underlying clips. This principle is frequently seen when television broadcasters display a static logo watermark in the corner of the screen. We can do the same with our example, adding an image with areas of transparency created in Serif DrawPlus and exported as a 32-bit PNG file.

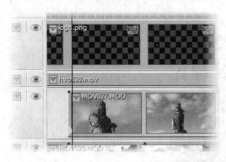

Timeline

Video preview

If you're looking to create an effect where your video is playing inside a picture—e.g., a billboard displaying your video—this can be achieved in two ways by:

- placing your video above a billboard image and shaping the video to match the billboard area using a transform envelope.

- cutting out the billboard region of the image using a photo-editing program such as Serif PhotoPlus (exported as a 32-bit PNG to maintain transparency) and placing it on top of your video, perhaps shaping your underlying video to match the billboard region using a transform envelope.

Both methods have similar results, but the second would allow some foreground objects in the image, such as a street sign, to sit in front of the billboard (see below).

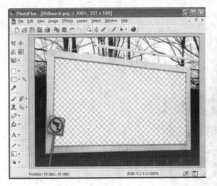

Image in Serif PhotoPlus

Video preview

Overlaid text

Text overlays are generally used for captions but can also include overlaid titles and credits. By adding a text clip to the upper video track, the text will be displayed in front of any underlying video. See Adding Text (p. 169).

Returning to our previous example, a caption could be added to describe the footage which is playing.

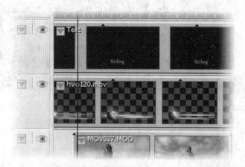

Timeline

Video preview

Top clip with reduced opacity

There are a number of ways to reduce the opacity of upper clips to partially reveal underlying clips—the quickest is to adjust opacity using the **Opacity** slider in the upper clip's Video track's Properties pane.

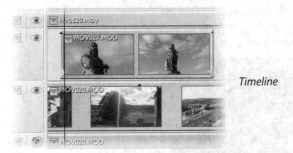

Timeline

*Video preview—
opacity set to 50%*

You can also adjust the opacity of a track (or even the clip itself) over time by manipulating its opacity envelope and associated keyframes. See Using envelopes and Adjusting keyframes)(p. 90 and p. 95) to learn how to modify envelopes by making keyframe adjustments.

Introducing transforms (timeline only)

Transforms allow you to resize your clips within the overall project size (which helps achieve picture-in-picture effects), to add perspective, and to scroll video, image, and CG clips (Backgrounds and QuickShapes) in any direction.

The possibilities are almost endless, because not only can you transform individual clips, you can also transform entire video tracks and even collections of video tracks in video groups.

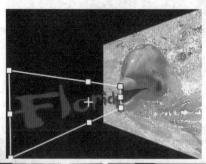

Several key techniques use transforms—here's a quick summary, using the above examples for reference:

Scaling and picture-in-picture
Scaling has been used in the second and third examples above; each video clip started at full screen size.

In the third example above, a picture-in-picture effect is created where a group of four videos is made smaller than the background video. It combines scaling and a new position, either static or animated.

Motion   Motion can be used, e.g. to position the text to the left in the first sample, and is illustrated by combining rotation and scaling in the third sample. Transform settings can collude to create video animation.

Perspective   Perspective has been applied to the "Florida" video in the first sample above.

Transforms all involve manipulation of the transform envelope, which you'll find discussed in Using envelopes (see p. 90).

5 Effects

Applying video effects

Effects can add variety and visual excitement to a video. Some effects, like **Brightness/Contrast** or **Gamma**, are designed to correct the original video; others, like **Filter Effects**, **Mosaic** or **Diffuse Glow**, are simply special effects.

The supported special effects are described as follows (see also effects for colour correction on p. 144):

- **Chroma Key** - A method of removing a colour (or a colour range) from one video to reveal another video or image behind it. The "removed" colour becomes transparent.

- **Colourize** - Offers an easy way to apply a colour tint/wash.

- **Diffuse Glow** - This broadens highlights in the video by brightening gradually outward from existing highlights.

- **Emboss** - The Emboss effect remaps contours to simulate a bas-relief effect. This creates a convex rounded edge and shadow effect.

- **Filter Effects** - Filter Effects encompass Shadows, Glows, Bevels, Emboss, Colour fills and 3D special effects. Apply individually or in combination.

- **Gaussian Blur** - The Gaussian Blur effect smoothes the image or video by averaging pixels. It's especially useful for removing a moiré (interference) pattern from scanned images and can help clean up regions of visual interference from fine patterns.

- **Gradient Map** - The Gradient Map adjustment is for remapping lightness information in the video to a new colour range. It makes for great "posterized" effects and is a quick substitute where a pop-art feel is being sought.

- **Greyscale** - This effect creates shades of grey; monotones ranging from black through to white.

- **Invert** - This effect inverts the colours, in the same way that a photo and its negative are opposites of each other.

- **Mask** - The Mask effect is a useful way to convert a clip into a more suitable mask by adjusting its lightness or other tonal values.

- **Mosaic** - The Mosaic effect creates blocks of uniform colour for a tiled appearance.

- **Motion Blur** - Exaggerate motion in your video, by blurring object movement.

- **Noise** - The Noise effect adds graininess.

- **Noise Reduction** - This removes unwanted graininess in your video, caused by poor environmental conditions, age of media, or poorly captured media.

- **Old Film** - Use the effect to simulate vintage film; control ageing and film quality.

- **Solarize** - The solarize effect is similar to a Negative Image function, but lets you set the threshold value above which colours can be inverted. (Solarization is a darkroom technique in which a partially developed image is re-exposed to light, producing dramatic changes in mid-tone regions).

- **Stabilize** - Use this effect to minimize camera shake present in your video footage.

- **Threshold** - The Threshold effect creates a harsh duo-tone black and white image, with no blend through shades of grey.

- **Unsharp Mask** - Unlike many sharpening tools that affect the entire video, the Unsharp Mask effect works mainly at edges. It's excellent for improving clip quality.

Audio special effects (see p. 147) can also be applied to audio clips.

Individual or cumulative effects can be managed from the Effects tab on the Properties pane. They can be added, replaced, deleted, edited, and rearranged all from this tab.

- Applied effects are shown in an effect list; effects at the top of the list are applied to the clip, track, or group first.

- When selected, an effects' properties can be adjusted directly in the pane.

- Any modified effect can be saved for future use.

Applying effects

To apply an effect:

1. Select the clip on the storyboard (or clip, track, or group on the timeline).

2. Click *fx* **Effects** on the context toolbar.

3. From the Properties pane (Effects tab), click ✚ **Add Effect...**.

4. From the dialog, choose a category (see explanations above) from the upper window. In the lower window, review the presets available (especially their names, which indicate their intended function). Select a preset.

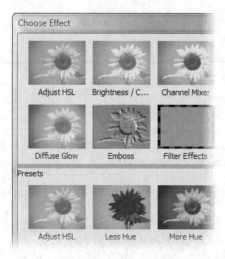

5. Click **OK**. The effect is added to the Effects tab's effects list.

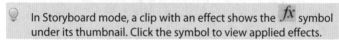

💡 In Storyboard mode, a clip with an effect shows the *fx* symbol under its thumbnail. Click the symbol to view applied effects.

Any effect added to your project will have its own set of properties associated with it. The effect's properties can be altered in the Properties pane (Effects tab).

To modify an effect:

1. Select the clip.

2. From the Properties pane (Effects tab), choose the effect to be edited from the effects list.

3. Alter the effect's properties (located at the bottom of the tab).

To save a modified effect to a new name:

- Click ![save icon] **Save**. Once named, the effect appears as a new preset in the appropriate folder in the Choose Effect dialog (or Video Effects tab in the Galleries pane).

Video effects on the timeline

The same principles as those described in Arranging tracks can be used when adding and combining video effects on the timeline, i.e. effects can be organized in the timeline's header region in a vertical sequence, composed from the top downwards just like video and audio tracks.

The timeline gives more powerful control of the effect over the duration of the clip or track, especially allowing for changes to the effect over time.

Applying effects over time

In Timeline mode, when an effect is applied to a clip, track or group, the object's **Attributes** button changes to grey /yellow (![icon]). The button, when clicked, lets you select the effect to reveal an Effects strip (you may need to scroll the timeline vertically) displayed directly under the object in the Keyframe View.

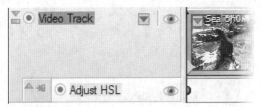

By clicking on a specific effect's keyframe (the ![button] button) at the start of the Effects strip, the keyframe properties for that effect can be adjusted so that the effect is modified for the duration of the clip, track or group (you can alter each keyframe's properties in the Properties pane under the **More** section).

While it's possible to apply an effect for the entire duration of a clip, track or group as discussed previously, it may be more effective for effects to be applied more sparingly over a specific, perhaps shorter, time duration. To do this you can use keyframes at different points. These keyframes are added along the clip's, track's or group's effect strip, and can each be modified in turn, to define how an effect's properties are to be applied at that point on the timeline. During playback, as the time indicator passes over each keyframe the clip will use the effect properties of the last visited effect keyframe. The effect can therefore be faded-in, faded-out, toggled on or toggled off.

Keyframe control is described in detail in Adjusting keyframes.

While it is not necessary to use effects groups in many cases, they are necessary if you wish to blend affected and unaffected video. This is extremely useful, as most effects do not offer "opacity" (strength of visibility) of their own. Mix back can be achieved by manipulation of the Video Effect Group envelope (see Using envelopes on p. 90).

See MoviePlus Help for more information.

2D filter effects

MoviePlus provides a variety of **filter effects** that you can apply to any clip with transparent regions (e.g., an overlay or CG QuickShape clips). The effect works on the edges of the visible portion of your image to offer shadows (below), glows, bevels, and emboss effects.

"3D" filter effects (see p. 141) let you create the impression of a textured surface and are covered elsewhere.

To apply 2D filter effects:

1. Select your clip and click *fx* **Effects** on the context toolbar, then from the Properties pane (Effects tab), click the **Add Effect...** button.

2. From the Choose Effect dialog, select the **Filter Effects** category and choose a preset from the lower window.

3. Click **OK**.

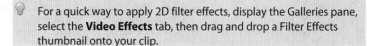

For a quick way to apply 2D filter effects, display the Galleries pane, select the **Video Effects** tab, then drag and drop a Filter Effects thumbnail onto your clip.

To edit a filter effect:

1. From the Properties pane (Effects tab), select "Filter Effects" in the effects list and click the **Edit Effects...** button. The **Filter Effects** dialog is displayed.

2. (Optional) Expand the preview pane by clicking the ▷ **Show/Hide Preview** button. When expanded, the effects are applied only in the preview window. While the pane is collapsed (click the button again), filter effects are applied directly to the clip.

3. To adjust the properties of the effect, select its name and vary the dialog controls. Adjust the sliders or enter specific values to vary the combined effect. (You can also select a slider and use the keyboard arrows.) Options differ from one effect to another.

4. Click **OK** to apply the effect or **Cancel** to abandon changes.

Creating outlines

MoviePlus lets you create a coloured outline around objects, especially text and shapes (as a **filter effect**). For any outline, you can set the outline width, colour fill, transparency, and blend mode. The outline can also take a gradient fill, a unique **contour** fill (fill runs from the inner to outer edge of the outline width), or pattern fill and can also sit inside, outside, or be centred on the object edge.

As with all effects you can switch the outline effect on and off. You'll be able to apply a combination of 2D or 3D filter effects along with your outline, by checking other options in the Filter Effects dialog.

Blur

Various blur effects can be applied to MoviePlus objects. The types of blur include:

*   **Gaussian**: the effect smooths by averaging pixels using a weighted curve.

*   **Zoom**: applies converging streaks to the image to simulate a zoom lens.

- **Radial**: applies concentric streaks to the object to simulate a rotating camera or subject.

- **Motion**: applies straight streaks to the object to simulate the effect of camera or subject movement.

3D filter effects

3D filter effects create the impression of a textured surface on any clip. You can apply one or more effects to the same clip—3D Bump Map, 3D Pattern Map, and 3D Lighting are all available. Some impressive effects can be achieved on a whole range of objects, particularly Text, Background and QuickShape clips.

Overview

To apply 3D filter effects:

1. Select a clip and click *fx* **Effects** on the context toolbar, then from the Properties pane (Effects tab), click the **Add Effect...** button.

2. From the Choose Effect dialog, select the **Filter Effects** category and choose a 3D preset from the lower window.

3. Click **OK**.

To edit a filter effect:

1. From the Properties pane (Effects tab), select "Filter Effects" in the effects list and click the **Edit Effects...** button. The **Filter Effects** dialog is displayed.

2. (Optional) Expand the preview pane by clicking the ▷ **Show/Hide Preview** button. When expanded, the effects are applied only in the preview window. While the pane is collapsed (click the button again), filter effects are applied directly to the clip.

3. Check the **3D Effects** box in the list (unless you've already selected a 3D preset). The **3D Lighting** box is checked by default.

✔ 3D Effects
  ✔ 3D Bump Map
    Function
      Advanced
  3D Pattern Map
    Function
      Advanced
  ✔ Transparency
  ✔ 3D Lighting

*   **3D Effects** is a master switch for this group, and its settings of **Blur** and **Depth** make a great difference; you can click the ⊞ button to unlink them for independent adjustment.

*   **3D Lighting** provides a "light source" without which any depth information in the effect wouldn't be visible. The lighting settings let you illuminate your 3D landscape and vary its reflective properties.

4. Once **3D Effects** is enabled (see Overview), adjust the "master control" sliders here to vary the overall properties of any individual 3D effects you select, i.e.

*   **Blur** specifies the amount of smoothing applied. Larger blur sizes give the impression of broader, more gradual changes in height.

*   **Depth** specifies how steep the changes in depth appear.

*   The ⊞ button is normally down, which links the two sliders so that sharp changes in Depth are smoothed out by the Blur parameter. To adjust the sliders independently, click the button so it's up.

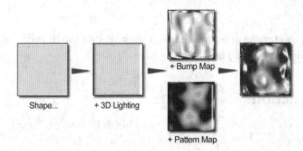

You can combine multiple 3D filter effects, as in the illustration above. The effects are applied cumulatively.

The procedures for applying 3D Filter Effects are covered in the MoviePlus Help but here's a quick review of each effect type.

3D bump map

The **3D Bump Map** effect creates the impression of a textured surface by applying a mathematical function you select to add depth information, for a peak-and-valley effect. You can use 3D Bump Map in conjunction with one or more additional 3D filter effects.

3D pattern map

The **3D Pattern Map** effect creates the impression of a textured surface by applying a mathematical function you select to introduce colour variations. You can use 3D Pattern Map in conjunction with one or more other 3D filter effects.

Transparency

The uniform transparency of a clip can be controlled via the **Opacity** setting in the clip's properties. However, for more sophisticated transparency control, especially for simulating reflective lighting effects, transparency settings can instead be set within the 3D filter effects dialog (check the **Transparency** option). Transparency can be adjusted independently for both non-reflective surfaces (typically a clip's edge shadows shown when side-lit) and top-lit surfaces.

3D lighting

The **3D Lighting** effect works in conjunction with other 3D effects to let you vary the surface illumination and reflective properties.

Colour correction

MoviePlus offers a wide variety of colour adjustment presets that you can apply to clips. These adjustments—to brightness, contrast, hue, and so on—are normally carried out on clips, as most deficiencies will be inherited from the recording of the clip (e.g., over-exposure, poor weather conditions, etc.).

Colour correction effects are applied and managed in the same way as for any other effect, i.e. go to the Properties pane (Effects tab), choose **Add Effect**, then choose an effect category thumbnail from the upper window of the dialog then a preset from the lower window (these change according to your selected effect category). Use the effect's Properties pane to alter the adjustment settings. See Applying video effects on p. 133 for more information.

Let's take a look at the colour adjustment effect categories in turn. Only some of the categories are related to colour correction.

Adjust HSL	Hue, Saturation, and Lightness (HSL) are components of a standard colour model that's used to identify colours. Generally speaking, Hue refers to the colour's tint—what most of us think of as rainbow or spectrum colours with name associations, like "blue" or "magenta." Saturation describes the colour's purity—a totally unsaturated video has only greys. Lightness is what we intuitively understand as relative darkness or lightness—ranging from full black at one end to full white at the other. Adjust HSL lets you alter these components independently.
Brightness / Contrast	Brightness refers to overall lightness or darkness, while contrast describes the tonal range, or spread between lightest and darkest values. This is a "quick and dirty" way of correcting a clip, for example one that was over-exposed or under-exposed.

Channel Mixer	The Channel Mixer adjustment lets you adjust each separate colour channel (Red, Green, or Blue) using a mix of all the current colour channels.
Colour Balance	The Colour Balance adjustment lets you adjust colour balance for general colour correction in the clip. Combinations of Cyan/Red, Magenta/Green and Yellow/Blue can be adjusted to lower or raise each colour mix.
Curves	The Curves adjustment lets you correct the tonal range of a clip—the spread of lightness values through shadow, midtone, and highlight regions—and control individual colour components.
Gamma	The Gamma adjustment lets you adjust the amount of mid-tone brightness in your clip. Think of midtones as the grey shading that lie between shadows and highlights present throughout your clip.
Levels	The Levels adjustment lets you emphasize mid-tone lightness regions in each or all of the three primary video colours, red, green, and blue.

Applying audio effects

In the same way that you can apply video effects to video clips, you can apply audio effects to audio clips also. In fact the process of applying and editing effects is identical for both—MoviePlus treats them equally.

Audio effects range from more commonly encountered effects such as Bass and Reverb, to more technical effects such as Low Pass, High Pass, Compressor, Expander, and many more.

Whichever effect you want to apply you'll need to have recorded, captured, or imported your audio file in advance; the file must also be present as a clip on your storyboard or timeline. Once present, the clip can have an effect applied.

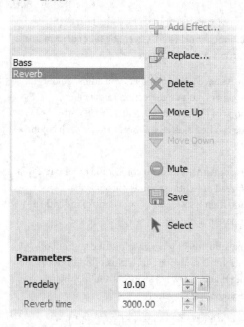

Individual or cumulative audio effects can be added and managed from the Effects tab on the Properties pane. They can also be replaced, deleted, edited, and rearranged all from this tab.

Parameters

Predelay	10.00	
Reverb time	3000.00	

- Applied effects are shown in an effect list; effects at the top of the list are applied to the clip first.

- When selected, an effect's properties can be adjusted directly under the list.

- Any modified effect can optionally be saved for future use.

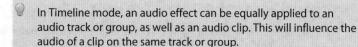

In Timeline mode, an audio effect can be equally applied to an audio track or group, as well as an audio clip. This will influence the audio of a clip on the same track or group.

Applying audio effects

To apply an effect:

1. Select the audio clip on the storyboard (or clip, track, or group on the timeline).

2. Click ![fx] **Effects** on the context toolbar.

3. From the Properties pane (Effects tab), click the ![+] **Add Effect...** button.

4. From the dialog, choose a category from the upper window. In the lower window, review any presets available (especially their names, which indicate their intended function). Select a preset.

5. Click **OK**. The effect is added to the Effects tab's effects list.

Any effect added to your project will have its own set of properties associated with it. The effect's properties can be altered in the Properties pane (Effects tab).

To modify an audio effect:

1. Select the audio clip, track or group which has the effect applied.

2. From the Properties pane (Effects tab), choose the effect to be edited from the effects list.

3. Alter the effects' properties at the bottom of the tab.

To save a modified effect to a new name:

*   Click ![save] **Save** in the Properties pane (Effects tab). Once named, the transition effect appears as a new preset in the appropriate folder in the Choose Effect dialog (or Audio Effects tab in the Galleries pane).

Using third-party effects

While MoviePlus is packed with a range of preset audio effects you can also adopt third-party **plug-in VST effects** (up to V2.4). If you've already downloaded such effects independently of MoviePlus you can make them appear in your Galleries pane by copying them to the MoviePlus install sub-folder called "VST". You'll need to do this before running MoviePlus. By default, this folder will be C:\Program Files\Serif\MoviePlus\X5\VST\.

The installed VST effects can be applied in exactly the same way as MoviePlus's audio effects—you can adjust their properties in the Properties pane (Effects tab). Note that some more advanced VST effects can be modified with a **VST Properties** button (in the same pane).

You can optionally store your VST effect plug-ins in a folder of your choice, but you'll have to point to this folder via **Tools>Options** (Folders menu option) for the effects to show in the Galleries pane.

 Installed VST effects are shown in the Galleries tab's Audio Effects tab in folders named with a [VST] suffix.

Applying audio effects over time

In timeline mode, you can change effects over time by adding and modifying keyframes along the timeline. See Applying video effects on p. 133.

Audio effect groups

While it is not often necessary to use audio effect groups, they can be used to mix multiple audio effects in and out of your project simultaneously. Groups are extremely useful as they offer a **Mix** setting; most individual effects do not offer mixing individually. This mixing can be achieved by manipulation of the Audio Effect Group (see Using envelopes). Such a group is created on an audio clip, track (below), or group by selecting **Audio Effect Group** from the **Insert** menu. Effects can be dragged into the group once created.

6 Audio

Introducing audio

In MoviePlus, it's possible to use audio clips which have been collected by a variety of methods.

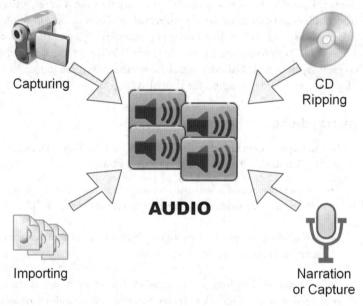

- Capturing audio: The capture process is capable of capturing just the audio element from a tape-based camcorder's combined video/audio input or audio from a microphone (see Capturing video on p. 28).

- Importing: You can make use of audio files already on your computer by simply importing them into your project.

- Recording Narration: Narrate commentary via microphone as you playback your movie. Narration can play back over existing audio (e.g., on a Music soundtrack).

- CD Ripping: Digital ripping of music CDs means that you can adopt your favourite songs as supporting soundtracks in your movie.

Whichever method you choose, audio files will be added to your Media pane. Narration files are also added to the storyboard or timeline automatically (at the time indicator position at which you started recording).

In many instances, the capture or copying of a video file from your respective tape- or file-based camcorder to your project will introduce accompanying audio along with your video clip automatically. For instance, copying an HD video file from your HD camcorder will add the file to your Media pane; the file normally contains separate but linked video and audio streams. When you introduce the file to the storyboard or timeline, the associated linked audio will follow.

Audio editing

Audio can play an essential part in any movie, and creative audio editing is an art in itself. Standard ingredients of audio might include:

- Production sound as originally recorded (and later captured) "in sync" along with the video, e.g. camcorder footage of your last holiday.

- Narration (or voice-over passages) which serves as a commentary or a bridge between sections of your movie.

- Theme music or background sound from a variety of clips, often added as one or more longer clips that run "under" audio narration.

- Sound effects or single-shot audio events, perhaps added for emphasis ("sweetening") or comic relief.

If you would like your movie to include more than basic production sound, allow yourself some time to do it right! Skilful sound editing is a combination of technique and judgment. Fortunately, MoviePlus makes the technical part straightforward. Getting sound to coincide properly with the visual track, to come in on cue and end (or fade out) at just the right moment, to blend well with other audio... all are easily accomplished in the Timeline mode.

Adding audio

123.WAV

Audio files can be added to your Media pane in various ways (see Introducing audio on p. 151) and will always show with an audio icon as a thumbnail. If capturing, the default prefix is "Capture".

Once in your project you'll want to add one or more audio files them to either your storyboard or timeline. One exception is when you're recording narration as the narration clip will be added automatically to storyboard or timeline.

 Use the Trim on the media pane to trim your audio file in the same way as a video file.

Adding audio to the storyboard

If the storyboard is empty, drag your audio clips so that they snap onto either the horizontal Narration or Music strips at the bottom of the storyboard.

You'll see a orange strip (indicating selection) appear under the thumbnails which indicates the audio clip. Click away from the clip to deselect it (it turns blue; below). The audio clip snaps to the start of any clip.

123.WAV

The clip is selectable and as such has its own properties (i.e., Gain and Pan) which can be adjusted (via the Properties pane). See Volume and pan on p. 160.

Adding audio to the timeline

Whenever you add a video clip with an audio component to the timeline, the audio portion (if present) is automatically added to an available audio track underneath the video track. These two clips maintain a linkage by default, as shown when you select either clip—an orange border indicates the current selection, while a light blue border indicates the linked accompanying clip.

However, when you add a standalone audio file (wav, wma, mp2, mp3) it can be dragged onto the available Music track (or you can create your own audio track).

Audio tracks are managed in much the same way as video tracks, and by the same token, audio clips are managed as for video clips. See Adding and arranging tracks and Arranging clips on p. 71 and p. 78, respectively, for more information.

In terms of playback, the audio clip is treated as for a video clip—seek controls can be used, along with trick play and scrubbing.

Audio waveform displays (Timeline mode only)

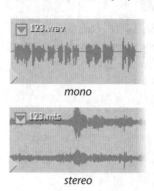

mono

stereo

Audio Waveform Displays provide a visual indication of the audio's dynamic range along the clip's length—typically used to spot cues and any unforeseen audio events. The waveform shows over the audio clip instead of a poster thumbnail as seen on video clips.

Note that the waveform display does not reflect the audio volume, as volume
and dynamic range represent two different elements of audio. If you increase the
volume the dynamic range does not change (and vice versa).

Waveforms are not generated automatically when your audio is added to the
timeline. Instead you generate audio waveforms as you require them on the
audio track.

To generate waveforms for audio clips:

- On the audio track's header, click the  **Minimize/Restore** button.

The audio waveforms for all clips on the track are generated.

The waveform displays can be hidden again by clicking the
Minimize/Restore button in the track header.

To switch off waveform generation:

- In **Tools>Options>General**, uncheck **Generate audio waveforms
  automatically**. When you restore an audio track, waveforms are no
  longer generated.

 If you've already generated waveforms for clips they will still display.
As waveforms are actually stored in waveform files (per clip) you'll
need to delete these waveform files in Helper File Manager on the
File menu.

Even though you may have switched off waveform generation, you can still
generate waveforms per clip.

To generate a waveform per clip:

- Right-click an audio clip and select **Generate Waveforms**.

 You can generate waveforms before adding clips to the timeline by
right-clicking your clip in the Media pane and selecting **Generate
Waveforms**. This avoids having to process all waveforms
simultaneously when adding to the timeline/storyboard.

Interpreting waveforms

The following example waveform shows a typical stereo waveform display. You can interpret your waveform by analysing peaks in the dynamic range indicative of passages of conversation and audio events (shouting, gunshots, bangs on the microphone, etc.).

By being alerted to these, you can perform audio trimming and splitting more effectively.

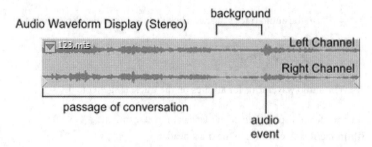

Audio fading (Timeline mode only)

In a similar way to video in/out transitions, any audio clip can have an audio transition. By default, when overlapping audio clips have been placed on the timeline (normally as a result of adding multiple video clips with accompanying audio clips) an **automatic** transition of type "Fade" is produced between overlapping audio clips. The transition smoothly blends the first clip's audio with the second clip's audio while maintaining the same audio levels throughout the transition's duration.

For non-overlapping audio clips, perhaps at the start or end of the timeline, a **manual** transition can be applied—this fades-in or fades-out an audio clip at the start or end of that clip, respectively. To apply, simply drag the blue triangular handle to the left (shown below) or right to produce the Fade transition. The length of the transition dictates the duration of the fade-in/out.

The duration of any manual Fade transition can be changed by dragging its handles or changing the **Duration** value in the transition's Properties pane. An automatic transition's duration can also be changed in the transition's Properties pane or by moving either clip in relation to the other (the automatic overlap defines the duration).

For automatic or manual transitions, you can adjust the **Interpolation** in the same pane—this alters the rate of change for the progression of the whole transition. The default is Linear, but other settings offer slow and/or fast beginnings and/or ends to the change.

Using audio buses

Audio buses are commonly encountered in professional music production for the control and management of audio tracks. By sending different audio tracks to different buses, the sound engineer has full control over how to "shape" the sound to his liking. In MoviePlus, the same logic can be applied to audio tracks in your project.

It is possible to use an audio bus to adjust overall gain (volume) and/or pan in your project. All audio tracks are directed by default to a single Master Bus, which can be modified to influence its associated audio tracks. Additional buses can also be created, allowing audio tracks to be directed to different custom buses.

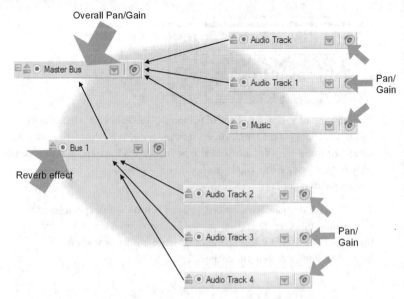

In the example above, independent Pan/Gain control of audio tracks is shown, with overall Pan/Gain control via the Master bus. The created custom Bus 1 can be used to apply an effect (e.g., Reverb) to audio tracks 2, 3, and 4.

Gain and pan adjustments, plus audio effects, can be applied to any bus. Envelopes are used to change the extent of Gain, Pan or effects over time; please see Using envelopes and Adjusting keyframes for more information.

Displaying buses

- Select **Show Audio Buses** from the **View** menu.

The Master Bus is displayed at the bottom of your timeline, along with any previously created custom audio buses.

Creating audio buses

●   Select **Audio Bus** from the **Insert** menu.

The new bus is added under the Master Bus at the bottom of your timeline, and is named Bus 1 or Bus 2, etc.

Modifying a bus

1.   Select the bus on the timeline, by clicking its name.

2.   From the Properties pane, alter properties (name, Gain, and/or Pan).

By default, all audio tracks are directed to the Master Bus. If you've created a custom bus, you'll need to direct the appropriate audio tracks to that new bus.

Assigning audio tracks to custom buses

1.   Select an audio track.

2.   From the Properties pane (Properties tab), select the chosen bus from the **Target** drop-down list.

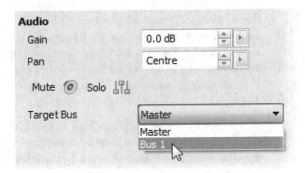

Volume and pan

Checking audio levels

The **Levels meter** can be used to study project-wide volume and pan settings, and to help you to attain optimum volume and pan—this is just as essential to a well-designed movie project as hours devoted to video editing.

> The meter is hidden by default but can be switched on by selecting **Show Levels Meter** on the **Preview** menu. The meter is displayed on the Video Preview pane.

Two meters which shows the entire project's audio levels. The left and right meters represent the left and right stereo channels, respectively, and report the audio levels in decibels (dB).

The meter levels will increase and decrease according to the volume level at that point in the project's playback.

The concept of the Levels meter is straightforward—the levels will peak and dip according to currently played audio levels. You may have experienced this on music systems while recording.

At some point, the meters may indicate that excessive volume levels are being experienced, i.e. the levels go above 0 on any meter. This is known as **digital clipping** (also known as square wave clipping). It is vital that such clipping does not occur in your project, so you have to set the loudest part of your audio clip to peak below 0 dB (or face audio distortion).

How do you know when clipping occurs? At the top of the example meters opposite, you'll notice two numbers at the top of each meter. The values represent the maximum level or "high-watermark" for each channel if clipping occurs during the current playback.

Again using the example, the left and right channel have at some point during playback peaked at +7.1 dB. You can leave your project to play, then return to check for clipping— if no values appear in red then no clipping has occurred. This saves you from having to watch the entire project's playback!

 These values are always reset when playback is restarted.

Assuming you've managed to prevent any clipping from occurring, you have to then consider how the audio sounds when played on a target device (e.g. via the web or on a created disc). You should aim to peak your audio levels at approximately -20dB (used for professional digital audio).

The meters only gives an accurate indication of incorrectly set audio clips or tracks—whether high or low. The prime objective is therefore to resolve unacceptable volume levels which we'll look at next.

Adjusting volume

Volume adjustment of clips

The volume adjustment on any selected audio clip (or even video clip with audio stream) can be made by altering **Gain** in the object's Properties pane (shown under the **Audio** section). For example, the Gain can be reduced by dragging the slider to the left (from its default 0.0 dB position).

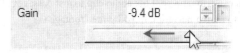

Adjusting pan

Adjusting the pan follows the same principles as adjusting volume. The adjustment can be made by altering **Pan** in the object's Properties pane (shown under the **Audio** section). For example, the pan can be reduced by dragging the slider to the left (from its default "Centre" position).

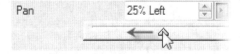

Adding narration

Narration means a passage of speech, normally an accompanying story (or a set of instructions), used to support the visual imagery of a movie.

In MoviePlus, narration is possible in either Storyboard or Timeline mode, by choosing the point from which to start recording your narration clip (set your time indicator first). As you play back your movie, you record your narration in real-time, then stop recording. The clip is automatically added to the storyboard or timeline, and is also added to the Media pane.

On the storyboard, the narration clip (Narration004) appears on the Narration strip under your thumbnails after you've stopped recording. See Storyboard basics on p. 43.

On the timeline, the narration clip (e.g. Narration003) is added from the set time indicator on a Narration track; the track is added automatically to your timeline, and can be manipulated as for any audio track.

See Volume and pan on p. 160.

For timeline narration, you can expand the Narration track to automatically generate audio clip waveforms (below), a visual representation of audio activity in the clip. In doing so, you can trim and split the audio clip to just passages of narration, making it easier to match narration to your video footage.

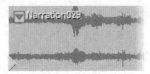

Setting up your microphone

Two microphone setups are likely: either a separate microphone and stereo headphones, or an integrated microphone in headphones. Devices may connect either via USB or via your computer's sound card (sometimes indirectly from your computer's front panel). Connected devices should be plug-and-play so don't need to be set up manually.

Most headphones are generally equipped with 3.5 mm jack plugs. Check the symbols on the jack plug then match these up with the same symbols on your computer's input sockets.

Consult your microphone documentation and Microsoft Windows for details on how to set up your audio device on your computer.

Recording

The Record Narration dialog lets you alter your recording setup (e.g., microphone clip) and start (and stop) the recording. During recording, a Levels meter indicates the current audio level.

To record a narration:

1. Move the time indicator in the Video Preview pane to a chosen recording start point (or select a clip on the storyboard to record from the beginning of that clip).

2. Click 🎤 **Record Narration** on the Storyboard or Timeline toolbar.

3. From the Record Narration dialog, optionally choose a different **Source** (e.g., "Microphone") if you have multiple audio input devices, an **Input**, or a different audio **Format**.

4. Speak into your microphone to check levels. If the volume is excessive, the Levels meter will show clipping (red areas showing at the top of each meter). To rectify, lower the 🔊 **Master Volume** slider until clipping no longer occurs.

5. Uncheck **Mute audio when recording** if you want existing audio to be played through your computer speakers (and picked up via microphone) as you record. Normally, you'll want to keep this checked to mute your audio as you record (or use headphones), to avoid "echoing".

Another source of echoing is when the Windows Volume Control outputs the microphone audio through the speakers, so it gets picked up by the microphone again (feedback). Avoid echoing in this case by use of headphones or by muting the microphone output.

6. To start recording, click the **Record** button and begin your narration. Click **Stop** button when you've finished speaking. If the end of the project is reached the recording will stop automatically. Your narration shows on your storyboard or timeline when you stop recording.

Click the **Windows Mixer...** button if you need to adjust MoviePlus volume levels from Windows.

Ripping audio discs

There may be occasion when you may want to adopt some of your favourite
audio for use in your MoviePlus project, whether as a complete song, piece,
narration, or as a smaller excerpt. If located on an audio CD, MoviePlus can use
ripping to capture each audio track sequentially; each track shows in your Media
pane after audio ripping. By default, tracks are saved as compressed wma files.

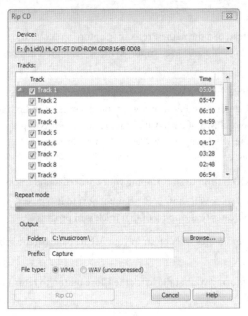

The dialog shows in-progress track-by-track digital ripping from an audio CD.
Track 1 is being ripped from the audio disc in drive F (and saved in
c:\musicroom\).

To rip an audio CD:

1. Click ![icon] **Import Media** on the **Tasks** toolbar or from the top of the
    Media pane.

2. From the drop-down list, select **Rip CD**.

3. From the dialog, choose a **Device** from the drop-down list; this is the
    disc drive currently containing your audio disc.

4.   (Optional) Use the playback controls under the track list to review tracks on your CD, e.g. use the ⊳ button to play a selected track. A bar under the play control buttons indicates the audio playback progress. For ripping selected track only, uncheck unwanted tracks from the list. Otherwise, all tracks are ripped.

5.   Use the **Browse...** button to specify a location that the audio files will be ripped to.

6.   (Optional) Instead of a file name **Prefix** of "Capture" enter your own prefix. MoviePlus will name each captured file with an incremented number suffix.

7.   (Optional) Enable the "WAV (uncompressed)" option, if you want uncompressed larger files. For wav rips, a typical 4 minute audio track will occupy about 40MB of hard drive space (typically 700MB per audio CD). Otherwise, keep the "WMA" option enabled to create smaller file sizes.

8.   Click the **Rip CD** button to start ripping your checked audio tracks. A currently ripped track will show a ⌃ symbol next to it; a green progress bar indicates that ripping of that track is in progress.

You'll notice that ripped audio files will appear in your Media pane (in the root of your Project tab).

When you've finished capturing your audio, click the **Close** button to return to MoviePlus.

7 Text, Images, and QuickShapes

Adding text

MoviePlus provides a high level of support for managing text in your project. Typically, text within MoviePlus can be used for titles, captions, or credits.

Titles
No movie is complete without initial titling to introduce the movie's name to the viewer.

Captions
Captions are always overlaid over an existing video or image clip, and display for that clip's duration. They are used to explain and provide context to the clip currently being displayed.

Credits
Credits tend to be closing credits, i.e. appearing at the end of your project, where you may want to acknowledge actors, and copyright information.

 Credits look great when animated!

However you plan to use your text, you create text as a **text clip**. This clip behaves much like a video clip but is purely a container for your text. You can position your clip on the same video track as your video clip, or above a video track for use as captions. By default, MoviePlus offers an **Overlay Track** on your timeline which is ideal for storing text clips as captions.

The text within your text clip is called a **text object**. A text object is a single instance of text which can be easily edited, when selected, using the following tabs on the text object's Properties pane.

- **Format**: Apply font type, font size, attributes, alignment, filter effects, and text styles.

- **Properties**: Control scrolling, playback and opacity.

- **Animation**: Make your titles and credits come to life—apply Blinds, Fly, Slide, Spin, and more.

- **Effects**: Include eye-catching special effects.

You can add additional text objects to your text clip at any time. Text clips can also have supporting images and QuickShapes added to them. (See Adding images and QuickShapes on p. 180.)

Titles

Titles are typically presented at the very beginning of your project. They tend to be a single word or at best only a few words long, but are usually shown in a large font size.

To add a title:

1. On the storyboard, select a clip (usually the first).
   OR
   On the timeline, set your time indicator's position.

2. From the **Insert** menu, select **CG Clip>Text**.
   OR

   Select **Add Text** from the Video Preview pane.

3. In the Video Preview pane, type directly into the text box to add you own title text.

4. Drag over the text to highlight and choose a preset text style from the Properties pane (Format tab) or choose your font type, font size, text alignment, font colour, transparency, line style and whether text is to be bold, italic and/or underlined. See Formatting text on p. 175.

Alternatively, you can use ready-to-go Titles presets from the Galleries pane (Titles tab); simply drag and drop onto your storyboard or timeline.

Captions

Captions are typically superimposed onto an existing clip to explain the underlying clip in text form. An example could be an overlaid title at the start of your project. For image clips, you could describe each photo's location, subjects in shot, etc.

To add a caption:

1. Select an existing video or image clip.

2. From the **Insert** menu, select **Caption**.
   OR

   Select **Add Text** from the Video Preview pane.

   In the Video Preview pane, you'll see default caption text added in front of the clip.

3. Type directly into the text box to enter your own caption text.

In Timeline mode, the caption text clip is added directly above the selected clip; both clips will be of equal duration. The Overlay Track, shown above all other tracks is intended to store your caption text clips.

 You can change a caption's start time and/or duration from the text clip's Properties pane (Properties tab).

In Storyboard mode, a clip with a supporting caption will show a Text icon under its thumbnail.

Credits

Credits are used to acknowledge cast and crew, as well as copyrights. They usually close a movie and tend to be presented on a neutral background (typically black). As a result, in MoviePlus it's best to present credits on their own text clip rather than as an overlay. This stops the viewer from being distracted by the underlying video clip.

A possible requirement when adding credits is the ability to display more than one frames worth of text (you may have a long list of cast, crew, and copyright information to acknowledge!). This is made possible by using **rolling credits**— the credits are made to move up, down, left, or right.

To add credits:

1. Deselect all clips on the storyboard
   OR

   Move the time indicator to the end of the last clip on your timeline.

2. From the **Insert** menu, select **CG Clip>Text**.
   OR

   Select **T₊** **Add Text** from the Video Preview pane.

3. Type directly into the text box selected in the Video Preview pane and edit as described on p. 175.

4. (Optional) To scroll overflowing credit text, set **Scrolling** in the Properties tab of the text clip's Properties pane—choose from Up, Down, Left, or Right. Set the **Duration** of the text clip to a value which allows credits to be read comfortably (the greater the duration the slower the credits).

Alternatively, you can use ready-to-go Credits presets from the Galleries pane (Titles tab); simply drag and drop onto your storyboard or timeline.

To import text from other Word processing packages, cut and paste directly into selected text in your Video Preview pane. For paragraphs, you'll need to add your own line breaks to set line lengths before copying.

Adding more text

It's easy to add a single passage of text by clicking and typing. However, MoviePlus can include more text, in addition to the initial text associated with the text clip. More text lets you build up additional subtitles, captions, or credits. Each text object is independent of each other and can therefore adopt its own format, properties, animation, or effect properties. The example below shows a title and subtitle, each possessing very different styles.

To add more text:

1. Select an existing text clip or video/image clip with overlaid text.

2. Click **T** **Add Text** on the Video Preview pane. An additional text box appears which can be edited as before. This creates a new text object associated with the original text clip.

Setting a default text style

If you've spent time creating the perfect text style and layout you might want to apply this to other text clips you subsequently create. This is done by making your chosen style the default style.

To set a default text style:

•   Right-click the text clip, and select **Set Default Text Style**.

The next text clip you create will be based on the text clip you chose as the default.

If you want to change an existing text clip which isn't based on your default, you can apply the new default to it.

To apply the default text style:

- Right-click the text clip, and select **Apply Default Text Style**.

Selecting and editing text

Text editing is possible only once text is selected—corner or edge control handles on the selected text's bounding box can be used for different operations.

Selecting text

For any text clip, click on the text you want to edit. A bounding box appears around the text once selected.

Click again for a insertion point where you can add additional text at that point.

To select only part of your text, drag over part of your text to select. Typing will replace the selected character.

Double-click on a word to select it.

Triple-click anywhere in the bounding box to select all text.

To select text objects, use the **Select** button on the Video Preview pane.

Editing text

To edit text:

1. Click on text in the Video Preview pane to select the text object.

2. Click again and type to replace all text (selected in purple).
   OR
   Drag over characters or words then type to replace highlighted text only (again shown in purple).

Use the **Edit** menu or keyboard shortcuts to access text editing operations such as Cut, Copy, and Paste.

You can format text from the Properties pane (Format tab).

To add a line break:

1. Click for an insertion point at the position where you want the line to break.

2. Press the **Return** key and continue typing.

Formatting text

MoviePlus lets you apply typical text formatting functions such as:

- Text formatting (font type, font size, attributes, alignment)

- Colour fill (solid and gradient) and transparency.

- Line weight and colour.

- Filter effects, such as drop shadow, glow, emboss, outlines, etc.

Instead of designing text styles from scratch you can adopt a text style preset from the Properties pane's Format tab instead. If needed, you can then customize text further by using the settings above the text style gallery.

To format text:

1. Select a text clip on the timeline (or an added text object in the Video Preview pane).

2. From the Properties pane's Format tab, you can alter (or apply):

   - **Font** (typeface), font size, text attributes (bold, italic, underline).

   - **Paragraph** alignment (left/centre/right).

   - **Fill** (solid or gradient colour). The swatch, when clicked, lets you apply a different preset fill (or edit a fill of your own). The swatch changes to reflect the text's current colour setting.

   - **Transparency** (solid or gradient). The swatch, when clicked, lets you apply a different Transparency preset (or a edit a transparency of your own). The swatch changes to reflect the clip's current transparency setting.

   - **Line**. When clicked, displays a Line Style dialog so that line weight and fill can be applied.

   - **Effects.** When clicked, a dialog for applying multiple 2D and 3D filter effects is displayed. 2D effects include shadows, glow, outline, bevel, emboss, colour fill, and feathering.

Add solid or gradient background colours to your text clip using **Fill** on the text clip's Properties pane (Properties tab).

The following examples show each 2D filter effect when applied to the letter "A."

Drop Shadow   Inner Shadow   Outer Glow   Inner Glow

Inner Bevel   Outer Bevel   Emboss   Pillow Emboss

Gaussian Blur   Zoom Blur   Radial Blur   Motion Blur

Colour Fill   Feather   Outline

See 2D filter effects (on p. 139) for more information.

Changing the line style:

- To adjust the currently selected text's line weight either drag the slider left or right or enter a point size value in the input box.

- For changes to Line fill, click the **Line fill** swatch to apply a different fill (or edit a fill of your own).

- Uncheck **Behind Fill** if you want the line fill to show over the top of your colour fill rather than behind it.

Animating text

Animation brings your text to life, creating titles, captions, or credits of great visual appeal. MoviePlus not only offers some familiar animations such as Zoom and Fade, Fly, Slide, Spin, and Explode but controls whether the animation is applied at the start or end of your text (or both). These are called **In Animations** and **Out Animations** and are key to understanding how to get the best out of your animations. As an example, the Out animation called Explode can be applied to the text clip containing the text "Animate".

Animation presets for In and Out animations can be applied from the context toolbar or from the Galleries pane. This saves you from having to create your own animation, although you're able to customize any presets and save the resulting animation for future use.

For text clips with multiple text objects:

- to apply the same animation to all text objects, apply the effect with no text objects selected.
  OR

- to apply independent animations to individual text objects, apply the effect with the text object selected.

To apply an animation:

1. Select a text clip (or text object).

2. Click **Animation** on the context toolbar.

3. From the drop-down list, pick either **Set In Animation...** or **Set Out Animation...** from the list (for a respective In or Out animation).

4. From the **Choose Animation** dialog, choose an animation category from the upper window. In the lower window, review the presets available for that category (especially their names, which indicate their intended function). Select a preset, e.g. Blinds.

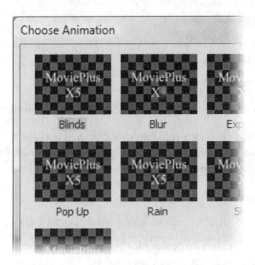

5. Click **OK**.

If you've already applied an In or Out animation, repeat the above procedure to apply the complementary Out or In animation, respectively.

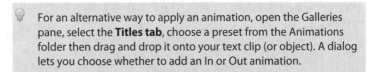

For an alternative way to apply an animation, open the Galleries pane, select the **Titles tab**, choose a preset from the Animations folder then drag and drop it onto your text clip (or object). A dialog lets you choose whether to add an In or Out animation.

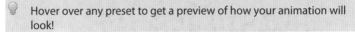

Hover over any preset to get a preview of how your animation will look!

Once you've applied animation, you can edit animation properties. As well as being able to check which animation is applied (and it settings), you can swap out one animation for another, alter its duration, and edit other animation-specific properties.

To edit an animation:

1. Select a text clip (or text object).

2. Choose **Edit Animations** from the context toolbar's
   Animation drop-down list.

3. From the Animation tab on the text clip's Properties pane, modify the
   In or Out animation.

To save your animation (Timeline only):

- From the text clip's Properties pane (Animation tab), expand In or

  Out Animation, click **Select**, then click ⊞ **Add to Gallery**. The
  animation will appear in the relevant folder under the Animations
  folder in the Galleries pane's Titles tab.

To delete an animation:

1. Select a text clip (or object) with the animation applied.

2. From the text clip's Properties pane (Animation tab), select **Reset** for
   the In or Out animation you want to delete.

Adding Images and QuickShapes

Images and QuickShapes can be added to your text clips to improve visual
appeal.

Once added, you can position, resize, rotate, transform, align, and order the image or QuickShape in relation to other objects. (See Manipulating objects on p. 182.)

Adding images

1. Select your text clip.

2. From the Video Preview pane, click **Add Image**.

3. From the dialog, locate and select the file to import, the click **Open**.

    The dialog disappears and the mouse pointer changes to the Image Size cursor. What you do next determines the initial size, placement, and aspect ratio (proportions) of the image.

4. Either:

    *   To insert the image at a default size, simply click the mouse.
        OR

    *   To set the size of the inserted image, drag out a region and release the mouse button.

    By default, the image's aspect ratio is preserved.

Adding QuickShapes

1. As above, but click **Add QuickShape** instead of **Add Image**. All QuickShapes are created initially as a square (or rectangle).

2. With the QuickShape selected, the Properties pane allows you to:

    *   swap the QuickShape to another QuickShape type, including Ellipses, Stars, Spirals, and Speech Bubbles.

    *   morph any QuickShape to create many different shape variations.

See Using CG Clips (p. 57) for more information.

Manipulating objects

The term **object** refers to any text, image, or QuickShape that you've added to your text clip. You'll typically add objects to enhance your titles, but you can add additional objects at any time as long as it is to a text clip.

These objects can be positioned, scaled, rotated, and transformed, as well as ordered and aligned—all from within the Video Preview pane.

 The examples below mainly involve text only, but the principles can be applied to text, images and QuickShapes equally.

Positioning
Drag a selected object around the pane into your ideal position.

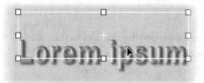

Scaling
Scale text by dragging a corner handle (this maintains aspect ratio). Drag with **Shift** key pressed for unconstrained scaling. By default, scaling is made in relation to the opposite corner (or edge) handle.

Instead, to scale from the origin point (   ), use the **Alt** key—drag edge handles to stretch and shrink.

Rotating
Hover over a corner—when the cursor changes to a Rotate cursor drag to rotate text.

   To rotate about a custom origin point, press the **Ctrl** key before dragging to move the origin point to a new position.

Shearing

With the **Ctrl** key pressed, drag an edge handle to shear.

Skew

Drag a corner handle with the **Ctrl** key pressed.

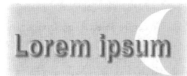

Ordering (Arranging)

To order a selected object in relation to other objects (by Z-order), right-click the object and choose **Arrange>** then one of the following options:

- **Send to Back**

  Sends the selected object to the back of the Z-order stack, behind all other objects.

- **Bring to Front**

  Brings the selected object to the front of the Z-order stack, in front of all other objects.

- **Back One**

  Shifts the selected object one position toward the rear in the Z-order stack.

- **Forward One**

  Shifts the selected object one position toward the front in the Z-order stack.

Aligning

To align multiple selected object in one operation and within their selection box, right-click the selected objects and choose **Align>**, then one of the following options:

- **Left**, **Right**, **Top**, **Bottom**: Aligns all objects to leftmost object, rightmost object, etc.

- **Horizontal Centre/Vertical Centre**: Aligns all objects to centre of the selection area (horizontally or vertically).

To centre object(s) horizontally or vertically in relation to their frame width/height, right-click on the selected object(s), and choose **Horizontally** or **Vertically** from the **Centre>** flyout.

8 Exporting

Exporting movies

There are a number of ways you can export your movie once you've edited it with MoviePlus... the project might look fantastic in your Video Preview pane, but there's likely to be an upper limit to how many people can crowd around your monitor and watch your preview, so you'll need to export your movie in a standard distributable format to allow others to share the experience!

The considerations you'll face when deciding how to export your project are the same for all video editors—the most important is "what device will the video be watched on and how am I going to deliver the video to the intended viewers?" This double-barrelled question, once answered, will help determine how you should export your movie for best results.

To play on:	You can:	Reference
computer (with CD)	create a Video CD (VCD)[1]	p. 188
DVD player (TV) **DVD drive** **(computer)**	create a DVD[1] create an AVCHD DVD[1]	p. 188
Blu-ray player (TV) **Blu-ray drive** **(computer)**	create a DVD[1] create an AVCHD DVD[1] create a Blu-ray Disc[2]	p. 188
iPad **iPod** **iPhone/iPod Touch**	Add to iTunes (for sync with Apple device)	p. 199
PSP	upload to PSP device[3]	p. 201
YouTube	upload to YouTube[4]	p. 202
Internet	standalone file	p. 198

[1] *Requires DVD Writer/Rewriter or CD Writer.*
[2] *Requires Blu-ray Writer.*
[3] *Requires a USB-connected PSP (set to USB mode).*
[4] *Requires a valid YouTube account.*

Exporting movies to disc

MoviePlus can export your project directly to disc (DVD, Blu-ray Disc, or VCD), producing a movie which will play on your TV or computer (via an appropriate disc player).

Optionally, you can create your own easy-to-navigate disc menus based on one of an impressive array of templates—all easily modifiable to suit your taste.

> For DVD/Blu-ray export, Dolby® Digital is used for audio encoding.

Disc settings

By default, MoviePlus will suggest the most appropriate export settings for your project, although you can alter these settings specifically for export if you have custom requirements. For example, PAL DVD and HD project settings are used directly for export settings in DVD and Blu-Ray disc creation.

Several stages make up the disc creation process:

1. Chapter point set up. If you want a menu on your disc, chapter points define locations in your project from which menu chapter thumbnails, when clicked, will begin playing the relevant video—much the same as the initial menu shown on any movie disc from your local movie store. See Using chapter points on p. 110.

2. Disc Setup. To setup basic and advanced disc settings. Includes Menu Designer, a template-driven tool to easily create optional disc menus.

3. Write Project. To initialize and create the disc.

The user is led through each stage seamlessly, culminating in the completion of your MoviePlus project.

To create a disc (using project settings):

1. Select **Export** on the **Tasks** toolbar.

2. From the drop-down list, choose a disc-related option (DVD, Blu-ray Disc, AVCHD, or VCD).

3. If you haven't already created a disc menu you'll be asked if you want to create one. If so, select Yes and the Menu Designer is launched.

Otherwise, the Export settings dialog is displayed (i.e., your disc will be menuless).

4. (Optional) From the dialog, choose a different export template from the list if needed. Normally, the already selected export setting is chosen by MoviePlus as the most appropriate settings and normally should be kept as is.

5. Click **Next>**.

6. From the Disc Settings dialog, review whether a **Disc menu** is required (check or uncheck as needed), and if necessary click the **Edit...** button to edit your menu in Menu Designer (see p. 190). The preview shows your currently selected menu.

7. (Optional) Check **Loop Playback** to make your movie start from the beginning after playback.

8. Use the **Disc Type** drop-down list to select your media. You can check that your project will fit intended blank media (e.g., DVD 4.7GB for DVD, BD-RE 25GB for Blu-ray Disc). Click **Detect...** to discover your writable disc drive(s).

9. Click the **Finish** button.

From the Write Disc dialog, choose a write **Speed** and **Drive** where your target media is located. Your completed disc will be ejected once the process is completed.

For subsequent disc creation, caching technology is used to speed up the process.

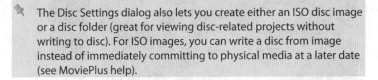

The AVCHD option lets you write HD projects to DVD.

The Disc Settings dialog also lets you create either an ISO disc image or a disc folder (great for viewing disc-related projects without writing to disc). For ISO images, you can write a disc from image instead of immediately committing to physical media at a later date (see MoviePlus help).

PAL vs. NTSC video standards

Whether you choose a PAL or NTSC template should depend on whether you intend for the video to be viewed in a PAL region or NTSC region. NTSC is the broadcast and recording standard used mainly in North and South American continents, plus parts of eastern Asia including Japan and South Korea. PAL is used widely throughout Europe, Africa, the Middle East, Asia, and Oceania.

Using Menu Designer

The Menu Designer is used for designing a disc menu, a navigational aid to easily access key points in your movie called chapters. Its user interface lets you design either your own menus from scratch or adopt a professional-looking template preset—choose either according to the extent of your design ability! Once your menu is complete, you can create your disc directly from Menu Designer.

The interface can be used to access template galleries, backgrounds, layout options, and much more, from a single Menu Bar. When selected, each bar's option offers a host of context-sensitive design elements appropriate to that option chosen.

Disc menus are also hierarchical, allowing main titles (e.g., Play Movie) to be placed on the top-level menu page, with other menu options (e.g., Scenes) able to be placed on a secondary-level page.

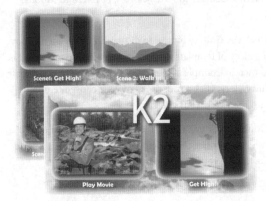

For movies with multi-page menus, typically for projects with many chapters, all pages can adopt the same design or each page can be designed differently. (See Creating multi-level menus on p. 196).

Once the disc is created the menu will display when the disc is loaded, allowing easy access to important parts of your movie. When viewing the movie on computer, simply navigate via mouse; for TV, use the remote control's navigation buttons to jump between disc menu's chapters and pages.

To launch Menu Designer:

- Click **Menu Designer** on the **Tasks** toolbar.

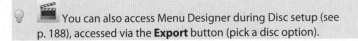

You can also access Menu Designer during Disc setup (see p. 188), accessed via the **Export** button (pick a disc option).

Galleries

To make life as simple as possible you can adopt one of a series of "themed" templates, stored in galleries such as Modern, Seasons, Funky, and Moods, amongst many others.

Gallery

Click the **Gallery** button to display an upper menu above a gallery of template presets for a selected menu item (as shown in example above). Choose a menu item, navigate the gallery, click a thumbnail of your chosen template, and then view your design.

Double-click on "Your Title" text and type your own disc title, then either close Menu Designer or, more typically, customize your template further.

Customizing a template

The Background, Layout, Title, Thumbnail, Buttons, and Labels buttons can all be used to modify your chosen template. By clicking any one of these options along the top bar the user interface refreshes to display an appropriate menu and accompanying gallery on the right-hand side of the Menu Designer workspace. For example, if you click Title, then a text-related menu will be shown above a gallery of title presets. Try it out by clicking on each button on the Menu Bar!

Background

Click the button to display an upper menu of background types above a series of gallery thumbnails for the selected menu item. You can choose from a gallery of solid or gradient colours, or from a range of artistic background images.

To import your own image or video for use as a background, click **My Image or Video**, then click the **Add** button. From the Open dialog, choose a media file to add to the background gallery—click the media file to apply it as a background.

Layout

Pick an accompanying layout which will house thumbnails for all chapters, either on a single or multiple pages. Thumbnails are arranged in rows, columns or in more artistic patterns. For example, a page layout with eight thumbnails would match perfectly with a movie with eight chapters.

If you choose a layout option with fewer chapter thumbnails than the number of chapters in your project you automatically create a multi-page disc menu. For example, a "4 Per Page" layout would create a two-page disc menu for a MoviePlus project with 8 chapters.

T

Title

If you want to change the attributes of your current title, click this button. The gallery will show a range of preset titles with various effects applied—some relatively modest, some downright flashy! Select a preset closest to the one you want to use. The titling will update on your main page to reflect the change.

If you want to then edit your title, use the menu to change the Font, Effects, Colour and Opacity of all your title characters.

The Menu Designer supports in-place text editing, which means direct editing of title text is possible. Either click on the title and type to replace the title text or type at a insertion point to add more text. You can perform all the common text editing functions such as copy (Ctrl+C), paste (Ctrl+V), and delete; you can also add a soft carriage return with **Ctrl**-Return.

Thumbnail

Select this button then choose the Frames or Shapes category. The latter offers shapes such as Ellipse, Star, Diamond, amongst others. Pick a preset from the lower gallery—a whole range of thumbnail shapes and styles are available. For shaped thumbnails only, change the thumbnail's Border Colour, Border Opacity, or apply Effects.

Label

Chapter thumbnail labels can be modified as described above for Titles. Note that the change affects all labels and not an individual label. In-place text editing is supported.

Buttons

Navigation buttons are used to navigate between multi-page disc menus. You can swap out the current buttons, especially if a colour clash occurs with your background (preset or imported). Click the button to reveal a gallery of buttons. Pick a button style, then select your chosen button colour from the menu above the button gallery.

Full Page

For multi-page menus, changes are made across all pages by default. If the button is disabled, changes are made to the current page only.

Preview

Click this button to view how your project will look like on your TV without the need to create a disc. Preview, adjust your menu design, then preview again until your menu is to your satisfaction. Use the accompanying buttons to simulate your DVD player's remote control for testing.

Editing chapter properties

When you launch Menu Designer, you'll see either:

- a single thumbnail called "Play" appear in your menu workspace. This occurs if you haven't inserted chapter points on your timeline.
  OR

- If you have inserted chapter points onto your storyboard or timeline (as part of video editing), a series of thumbnails are shown which represent the chapter at which you added a chapter point.

Once chapters are present, their properties can be edited or viewed, i.e. you can:

- preview the content of each chapter by playback.

- zoom in/out of individual frames to inspect the chapter.

- swap to a different thumbnail (taken directly from the frame at the chapter point position), e.g. a frame which typifies a chapter much more than any other.

- change the chapter name, i.e. the label shown next to the thumbnail.

To view chapters:

- Double-click a chapter thumbnail in the menu workspace.

In the Chapter Properties dialog, the video frames displayed for a chapter are those spanning between the selected and the next chapter point on the timeline (if no chapter point exists after the current one the remainder of the movie is shown).

The available navigation controls assist with the inspection, viewing and editing of the chapter.

To use a different frame as thumbnail:

- In Chapter properties, use the navigation controls to navigate then pick the right frame. Once you're happy with the thumbnail shown in the preview window, click the **Jump to Caret** button (this aligns the red **Image** indicator under the time indicator position). On exit, this thumbnail will now be shown to represent your chapter. OR

- Drag the red indicator, which realigns then synchronizes the time indicator to it. This automatic alignment provides a simple method for alternative thumbnail selection (avoiding the Jump to Caret operation).

Changing the thumbnail picture does not affect the chapter point positions on the timeline. However, moving chapter points on the timeline will reposition your modified thumbnail, so remember to always check thumbnails are correctly set.

To rename your chapter:

- In Chapter properties, enter a new **Name** (or edit the existing name).

Creating multi-level menus

In advance of entering Menu Designer, your chapter points need to be defined for your project. If you want to create multi-level menus, chapter points for your top-level menu have to be additionally set as "Top Level" chapter points. This is done from the Properties pane when your chapter point is selected—simply select the Top Level option, adding your own text if required.

All other chapter points without this option enabled are automatically relegated to lower-level menus.

For more information about chapter points, see Using chapter points on p. 110.

Setting background music

By default, no background music is played when your disc menu is displayed on your target device. However, it's often a nice finishing touch to complement your menu design with supporting audio—use it for instructional reasons or to simply play background music. The audio stream of a video file can also be used as a background music.

> If you've used a background video on your menu, you can use its audio as a page soundtrack. The same music can be applied to all pages or you can apply different music to the current page only using the **Apply to All** button.

To enable background music:

1. Click the **Page Setup** button on the Menu Bar.

2. From the dialog, pick an option from the **Music** section. Either:

   - For music from a **saved audio or video file:**
     Click the second radio button, and either type the path to the media file or click the ⋯ **Browse** button to navigate to the file. For the latter, navigate and select a media file (video file must contain audio) from the dialog. Common Audio files such as .MP3, .WAV, and .WMA are supported, as well as video files such as .AVI, .MPG, .MOV, .WMV and .ASF.
     OR

- For music from the **page's background video**:
  Enable the **Use soundtrack from background video** button. You must have previously set a video as the Custom Background from the same dialog.

3. Click **OK**.

Writing project

The Menu Bar hosts a ![button] button which displays a drop-down menu with options for writing to Blu-ray discs, AVCHD discs, DVDs, and VCDs directly from the Menu Designer.

Animating your menu

If your menu needs some extra visual appeal it's possible to animate your menu thumbnails or background, or both. This will automatically play movie chapters within their thumbnail preview, or play any currently configured video background.

To animate thumbnails and/or video backgrounds:

- In ![icon] **Page Setup**, check either **Animate Thumbnails** or **Animate Background**, or both. A slider sets the time the thumbnails or background will animate for before the animation loops and plays again.

Closing Menu Designer

- ![X icon] Choose **Exit Menu Designer** in the **Options** menu or click the **Close** button. You will be prompted to save your project if it is currently unsaved. Your updated template will be shown by default the next time you load the Menu Designer.

Exporting as a file

MoviePlus can export your project to one of several commonly encountered video file formats.

> Which type of file do you want to export?
>
> MP4 Video (*.mp4)
> MPEG Video (*.mpg;*.m2ts;*.m2t)
> QuickTime (*.mov)
> Windows Media audio and video (*.wmv)
> Video for Windows (*.avi)
> Windows Media audio (*.wma)
> Waveform audio (*.wav)

In most instances, you would export your file as an MP4 Video (*.mp4), unless there is a specific reason for choosing a different export option. The MP4 format is a modern compressed streaming format (utilizing the H.264 video codec), ideal for Internet use and storage on both local and portable devices.

To export as a file:

1. Select the **Export** on the **Tasks** toolbar.

2. From the drop-down list, choose **File**.

3. Select your chosen file type from the list according to intended use, then click **Next>**.

4. From the Export Settings dialog, several options are available:

   - (Optional) Select a preset export template (choose from Normal or Widescreen templates). Click **Customize...** to create your own export template if necessary.

   - (Optional) Change **Render Quality** (between Draft and Best quality) to control the level of video and audio processing carried out during export.

- (Optional; timeline mode only) If you're exporting just part of your project, the **Export selected range** option can be checked to limit the export; you need to place selection markers on your timeline first.

5. Click **Finish**.

6. To save the file, locate a target folder and specify a name for your file in the **File name** box, then click the **Save** button. Your project will then be composed and converted into the specified format and you will be shown a progress bar during this process.

7. On completion, the file can be opened with the **Open** button (to play the resulting video in your default media player software), you can explore the file's folder with **Open Folder** or just **Close** the dialog and return to MoviePlus.

 You can click **Cancel** to abort the export process (you'll be prompted to confirm this in case of an accidental key press and be offered to delete the file).

Exporting to iTunes/PSP

MoviePlus allows you to share your finished movie via Apple devices (iPad, iPhone4, and video-capable iPod devices). By exporting directly to iTunes you'll be able to include your movie in your iTunes library; simply sync up to your Apple device and your movie is ready to be shared.

You'll also be able to upload your movie to Sony PSP devices.

Export to iTunes

Exporting your movie to video-capable Apple devices is carried out in two stages—exporting the movie **automatically** to iTunes and subsequently syncing the movie to your Apple device. MoviePlus takes care of the first stage, but you'll need to sync your movie to your device as you would for any other movie file.

To export to iTunes:

1. Select the ![icon] **Export** on the **Tasks** toolbar.

2. From the drop-down list, choose **iTunes/PSP**.

3. From the dialog, select an export setting from the list for the intended Apple device, choosing an appropriate video standard (PAL or NTSC), quality level and optional Widescreen support.

   You can click **Customize...** to create your own export template.

4. Change **Render** quality—set **Draft** when testing and **Best** for final, high quality.

5. If you're exporting just part of your project, the **Export selected range** option can be checked; you'll need to place selection markers on your timeline first. See Using selection markers on p. 111.

6. Click **Finish**.

7. From the **Save As** dialog, locate a target folder and specify a name for your mp4 video file in the **File name** box, then click the **Save** button. Your project will then be composed and converted into the specified format; you will be shown a progress bar during this process.

   You can click **Cancel** to abort the export process (you'll be prompted to confirm this in case of an accidental key press and be offered to delete the file).

8. On completion, the file can be opened with the **Open** button (to play the resulting video in your default media player software) or you can explore the file's folder with **Open Folder** (or just **Close** the dialog and return to MoviePlus).

9. Click **Continue** to launch iTunes automatically. Your movie will already be added to your iTunes library (under Films).

The next time you connect your Apple device, it will sync up to your iTunes library, copying your movie to your device.

via PSP

If you own a Sony PSP, you can export your movie easily. In USB mode, your PSP is seen as any other removable storage device—as such your movie is uploaded onto the device with the minimum of fuss.

> To upload, your PSP **must** be in USB mode.

To export to PSP:

1. As for exporting via iTunes (above) but instead of choosing an Apple device export template, choose a PSP-specific template from the list. Click Next>.

2. From the **Upload to PSP** dialog, enter a **Movie title** and select the PSP device from the drop-down menu. This should show the PSP as a removable storage device.

    Select a PSP to upload to:

    H: (Sony PSP USB Device)

3. (Optional) Check **Keep a local copy...** to save the exported movie for use again (leads to quicker exports for unchanged projects).

4. Click **Finish**. The project will then be composed and converted into the specified format and you will be shown a progress bar during this process.

> You can click **Cancel** to abort the export process (you'll be prompted to confirm this in case of an accidental key press and be offered to delete the file).

5. Click **Continue** to upload the local movie up to the PSP.

Exporting to YouTube

You may have been aware of the mass popularity of video hosting sites, notably YouTube, in recent years. Placing a movie on YouTube means that you can share a short movie worldwide without writing to media or uploading to your own web site. The two-stage process involves exporting a file optimized for upload (i.e., wmv) then uploading the file to the YouTube website.

> 💡 A working YouTube (or Google) login is required to upload your movie to YouTube. If you don't have a login, visit www.youtube.com and register!

To export to YouTube:

1. Select **Export** on the **Tasks** toolbar.

2. From the drop-down list, choose **YouTube**.

3. From the dialog, select a YouTube export setting from the list. A low quality setting will create a lower quality movie by reducing the Video bit rate on export.

    You can also click **Customize...** to create your own export template.

4. (Optional) Change **Render** quality—set **Draft** when testing and **Best** for final, high quality.

5. (Optional) If you're exporting just part of your project, the **Export selected range** option can be checked; you'll need to place selection markers on your timeline first. See Using selection markers on p. 111.

6. Click **Next>**.

7. From the **Save As** dialog, locate a target folder and specify a name for your wmv video file in the **File name** box, then click the **Save** button. Your project will then be composed and converted into the specified format and you will be shown a progress bar during this process.

8. You can click **Cancel** to abort the export process (you'll be prompted to confirm this in case of an accidental key press and be offered to delete the file).

9. (Optional) On completion, the file can be opened with the **Open** button to check before YouTube upload (this plays your video in your default media player software) or you can explore the file's folder with **Open Folder**.

10. Click **Continue** to launch the YouTube Upload dialog. Add your YouTube login details (UserID and Password), movie **Title** and **Description**, a YouTube Video **Category**, and some keywords (**Tags**) for users to search for.

Instead, you can upload by using valid Google account details (but you'll still need a valid YouTube UserID also).

11. Click **Finish** to begin the file upload. A progress bar is shown during upload.

9 Appendices

Performance Notes

While MoviePlus has been engineered from the ground up to provide a fast working environment, video editing is still a task that demands a great deal from a typical computer. The amount of data being moved between the system's hard drive, memory, and processor (and back again) can be immense, stretching the capabilities of many PCs. At the same time the system processor (CPU) has to perform the additional task of visual effects processing and composing your edited clips into a resulting movie.

There are several techniques used for improving playback performance as well as computer performance checks to help optimize your computer for video editing. The former involves pre-rendering and proxy file generation (for HD video); the latter will help overall speed, but in particular will help with data-intensive operations like composing and exporting a movie with MoviePlus!

Improving playback performance

For non-HD projects, you may not experience any playback problems during preview. However for more complex projects, i.e. those using a myriad of special effects or transitions on multiple tracks, or HD projects you may encounter **stuttering playback**. Several options can be used to alleviate this:

- Dropping the Render Quality during preview

- Pre-rendering (a clip, transition, or time range)

- Creating proxy files (if using HD video)

You can adopt a combination of these methods to suit your project.

Render quality

The **Render Quality** setting on the **Preview** menu (or right-click on the Video Preview pane) determines at what quality your movie will be previewed and will determine how hard MoviePlus will work to draw (render) your movie. Quality options range from Draft to Best—if you are experiencing stuttering playback, especially where transitions or effects are in progress, you can reduce the preview quality to improve playback speed without harming your project.

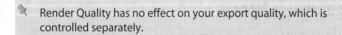

Render Quality has no effect on your export quality, which is controlled separately.

You can also improve playback performance, by reducing the size of your preview (zoom out) by clicking the **Zoom Out** button (or via the same option on the Preview menu).

Pre-rendering

Pre-rendering can be enabled in advance of video preview to **improve playback performance**, especially when displaying transitions, effects, blending, and text. It can take place in several ways—either for your entire project, for specific clips, on one or more multiple transitions, or over a set time range.

When you drag clips onto your timeline, you'll see red pre-render indicator bars (arrowed below) above your timeline ruler to show areas which are suggested for pre-rendering (in the example below, transitions between clips are suggested for pre-rendering).

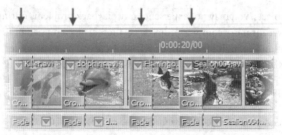

Once you've pre-rendered your project (discussed later), these red bars will change to green bars.

If pre-rendering is in progress, the indicator bars for the portion of your project currently being pre-rendered shows temporarily in orange.

Pre-rendering is a background task, which allows you to get on with your project development. The process actually creates preview files which can be managed and deleted.

Pre-rendering is also a cross-track operation; all objects on all tracks within the red indicator bars will be pre-rendered.

A green progress bar on the Status Bar indicates pre-rendering progress. Pre-rendering may take some time to complete for larger files. If needed, you can click the **Cancel** button on the bar to abort the process.

A standard location is used to store pre-rendered files. This location can be viewed or changed from **Tools>Options>Folders**—you can click the **Browse...** button to select a different **Pre-rendered video folder** location.

To pre-render your entire project:

- Right-click the Video Preview pane and select **Pre-render All**.

The Status Bar indicates pre-rendering of your project. Once complete, pre-rendering will have changed any red indicator bars to green.

As you further develop your project—changing transitions, adding clip effects, adding text clips, performing video blending—you'll see red indicator bars again. Don't panic! You just need to pre-render your project again!

MoviePlus lets you pre-render complex areas of your project in isolation (if you've got a particular reason to do so).

To pre-render clips or transitions:

1. (Optional) Select one or more clips or transitions on the timeline. For all transitions, right-click and pick **Select related objects**.

2. Right-click on the object(s) and select **Pre-render**.

For a time range, you'll have to insert and position Start and End selection markers on your timeline (p. 111).

To pre-render a time range:

1.   Click on the timeline ruler to set the time indicator's position.

2.   From the context toolbar's **Markers** drop-down menu, choose **Set Selection Start** (or right-click on the time indicator) to set the start of your time range. From the same menu, select **Set Selection End** to set the end of your range.

3.   (Optional) Drag your **Selection Start** and **Selection End** markers along the timeline to fine-tune your time range.

4.   Select **Pre-render Selected Range** from the **Preview** menu (or right-click on the Video Preview pane).

The **Preview** menu also lets you temporarily switch off pre-rendering (uncheck **Use pre-rendered video**) or delete any previously rendered preview files (**Clear pre-rendered video**). Preview files can also be deleted via the **Helper File Manager**. (See Managing helper files on p. 212.)

Using Proxy files

A proxy file in MoviePlus is a reduced-resolution file which is written to assist in the playback of your HD video clip, therefore optimizing the program's playback performance. Otherwise, previewing a HD video clip will put extra demands on your computer's processor due to its high resolution characteristics, resulting in stuttering playback.

Proxy files are created by default when you drag HD media onto your timeline/storyboard. You'll see a progress bar on the Status Bar showing each proxy file being created for each HD video clip in turn.

For computers with quad-core processors, previewing HD video smoothly is a reality. As a result, proxy file generation in MoviePlus when using such computers is disabled by default. For some higher performance computers, you may not need to proxy your HD video files as your computer may be sufficiently powerful to preview acceptably. This can be disabled from **Tools>Options...** if needed.

To switch off proxy files automatically:

1. Select **Options...** from the **Tools** menu.

2. From the **Proxy Files** menu option, uncheck **Use proxy files for HD video**.

 You can always temporarily check how the original file plays back at any time by right-clicking your file and unchecking the **Use Proxy File** option prior to previewing.

Instead of creating proxy files automatically, you can create proxy files for specific HD video files directly on the storyboard (timeline).

To create a proxy file for a single HD video clip:

*   Right-click on the HD video clip (timeline only), and select **Use Proxy File**.

You have the option of creating proxy files in the Media pane before committing HD video clips to the timeline/storyboard. Right-click a clip and choose **Create Proxy File**. This avoids having to generate lots of proxy files sequentially as you add HD video clips to the timeline.

Proxy files are not removed on exiting MoviePlus. If you're worried about disk space usage you can:

- Delete the proxy files via the **Helper File Manager** (see below).

- Change the standard folder location used to store proxy files. This location can be viewed or changed from **Tools>Options>Folders**— you can click the **Browse...** button to select a different **Proxy files folder** location.

- From **Tools>Options>Proxy Files**, use a different Codec for encoding proxy files. WMV or MPEG codecs offer reduced proxy file sizes.

Managing helper files

Helper files comprise a range of file types, such as pre-rendered preview files and proxy files, that are created as background tasks to optimize MoviePlus performance. Files for indexing, scene detection, audio waveforms, and motion (Image Stabilization) are also considered helper files.

All of these file types can be generated as **background tasks** at different times in your project. The **Background Task Manager** (**File>Background Tasks...**) displays these files while being processed.

Once generated, the helper files can be displayed and, if needed, deleted from one location, called the **Helper File Manager** (**File>Helper Files...**).

To delete helper files:

1. Click **Helper Files...** on the **File** menu.

2. From the Helper File Manager dialog, select the relevant option in the drop-down list. For example, choose **Preview files** or **Proxy files** when deleting pre-rendered files or proxy files, respectively.

3. Select an individual preview file in the list and click **Delete**. Alternatively, click **Select All**, then **Delete** to remove all preview files.

4. Click **Close**.

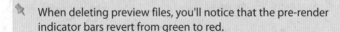

When deleting preview files, you'll notice that the pre-render indicator bars revert from green to red.

Improving system performance

Disabling Anti-Virus on-access scanning/live protection

Many anti-virus programs offer a live virus-checking service running in the background, often called auto-protect, active shield service, or on-access scanning. This increases the level of security offered by your PC as all files being accessed are checked for viruses instead of waiting for a full system scan once a week to know you're safe, but this of course does slow down disk access for other programs. If MoviePlus performance is not as you expect, it might be worth investigating your current auto-protect or on-access virus scanning settings as they may be affecting disk performance while using MoviePlus.

Using a fast drive

To optimize the speed of access to your MoviePlus project files and project clips you should use a dedicated fast drive if possible.

You should also avoid using an external disk drive as the location for your project and its clips. External drives will affect disk access times and impair video preview playback.

Windows swap file location

If you are a power user familiar with the Windows swap file or virtual memory settings, you may like to consider moving your swap file location to a drive other than the one used to store or process your video. This may help improve performance when Windows is using your virtual memory in complex compositions or exports. This should be carried out at your own risk.

Disk defragmentation

A defragmented drive or dedicated empty drive is preferred for video editing work.

You can defragment your drive using a built-in Windows tool, normally available by right-clicking a drive in Windows Explorer and choose **Properties**, the **Tools** tab, then click **Defragment Now....**

PC processor performance

While it may not be necessary to upgrade a computer in order to run MoviePlus, there are some things to bear in mind in the event of a new PC purchase or upgrade, if your video editing warrants the attention.

- If you're considering upgrading to a HD camcorder, and are expecting to create HD projects natively you need to consider using a computer with a quad-core processor.

- If you're upgrading to a computer with a dual-core processor, you may need to proxy files for HD operation. You may need to experiment with HD video playback with and without proxy file support. See Using proxy files.

Memory requirements

Consider upgrading your RAM if you plan to work on projects involving HD video. Increasing RAM will also improve MoviePlus performance on larger projects generally. See System Requirements on p. 14.

Keyboard Shortcuts

 These published shortcuts are the program default shortcuts. However, it is possible to customize these to fit your own requirements, invalidating this information.

Single-letter keys	Description
G	Group
I	Set Start Time
M	Mute
O	Set End Time
S	Split
Control Keys	**Description**
Ctrl+Shift+C	Copy Frame in Preview
Ctrl+Shift+F	Autofit
Ctrl+Shift+F	Destroy Group
Ctrl+Shift+0	Zoom Preview to 100%
Ctrl+Shift+Left	Go to Previous Marker
Ctrl+Shift+Right	Go to Next Marker
Ctrl+Left arrow	Moves track out of group (Timeline mode)
Ctrl+Right arrow	Moves track into group (Timeline mode)
Ctrl+Up arrow	Move track or group up the stack (Timeline mode)
Ctrl+Down arrow	Move track or group down the stack (Timeline mode)
Ctrl++	Zoom in to timeline
Ctrl+-	Zoom out of timeline
Ctrl+[	Zoom to all (timeline)

Ctrl+]	Zoom to Selection (timeline)
Ctrl+<	Select Previous Keyframe
Ctrl+>	Select Next Keyframe
Ctrl+\	Switch to Timeline (Storyboard) mode
Ctrl+A	Select Related Objects
Ctrl+C	Copy
Ctrl+Delete	Delete Selection Only
Ctrl+Home	Scroll to Time indicator
Ctrl+M	Go to Marker (or chapter point).
Ctrl+N	New MoviePlus Project
Ctrl+O	Open MoviePlus Project
Ctrl+P	MoviePlus Project Settings
Ctrl+S	Save MoviePlus Project
Ctrl+V	Paste
Ctrl+X	Cut
Ctrl+Y	Redo
Ctrl+Z	Undo
Ctrl+1	Draft Render Quality
Ctrl+2	Preview Render Quality
Ctrl+3	Normal Render Quality
Ctrl+4	Good Render Quality
Ctrl+5	High Render Quality
Ctrl+6	Best Render Quality

Misc keys	Description
Del	Delete
End	Go to end of movie
Esc	Stop the movie (and return to start of playback)
Home	Go to start of movie
Left	Go to Previous Frame
Right	Go to Next Frame
Space	Play/Pause the Movie

Function Keys	Description
F1	Help
F5	Starts/stops video playback
F6	Inserts a marker
F7	Inserts a Video Effect
F8	Inserts a Video Effect Group (Timeline mode)
F9	Inserts a Video Track (Timeline mode)
F10	Inserts an Audio Track (Timeline mode)
F11	Inserts a Video Group (Timeline mode)
Ctrl+F12	Inserts an Audio Bus (Timeline mode)
Shift+F6	Inserts a chapter point

Shift Keys	Description
Shift+F	Align to Frames
Shift+G	Remove from Group
Shift+L	Linking (Timeline mode)
Shift+P	Move time indicator to end of clip when pasting
Shift+R	Rippling
Shift+S	Snapping
Shift+Left	Go to Previous Clip
Shift+Right	Go to Next Clip